$3 Soups and Stews

Delicious, Low-Cost Dishes for Your Family That Everyone Will Love!

Ellen Brown

Lyons Press
Guilford, Connecticut
An imprint of Globe Pequot Press

Soups and stews are the epitome of "wet heat," so this book is dedicated to my dear friend Nick, who shares my passion for this genre of cooking.

Lyons Press is an imprint of Globe Pequot Press.

Text design: Sheryl P. Kober
Project editor: Julie Marsh
Layout artist: Melissa Evarts

Library of Congress Cataloging-in-Publication Data

Brown, Ellen.
$3 soups and stews : delicious, low-cost dishes for your family that everyone will love! / Ellen Brown.
p. cm.
Includes index.
ISBN 978-1-59921-892-2
1. Soups. 2. Stews. 3. Low budget cookery. I. Title. II. Title: Three dollar soups and stews.
TX757.B76 2010
641.8'13—dc22

2009034426

Printed in the United States of America

10 9 8 7 6 5 4 3 2 1

Contents

Preface

Yummy comfort foods satisfy so many of our needs. They bring us both psychological and physiological satisfaction. They nourish both our bodies and our souls. Comfort foods are not "edgy" or challenging; they don't contain harsh contrasts like vinegar on fresh strawberries. They make us happy.

A bowl of steaming soup on a cold winter's night is the edible equivalent to the favorite stuffed animal or beloved "blankie" of our childhoods. The aroma coming from a plate of chunky stew conjures rosy memories of blowing the white puffs off the tops of dandelions in fields and the excitement of anticipating trick-or-treating on Halloween.

Comfort foods are easy-to-prepare, straightforward, and honest recipes. There is no fondling of the food to create a sunburst from snow peas or a swan from spun sugar when you're making comfort foods. What we term "comfort foods" are frequently called "nursery foods" in England due to their simplicity, and every cuisine and culture has recipes for these appealing treats. It might be a bowl of clam chowder to a native of Boston, but it's a bowl of congee to someone born in Beijing.

Psychologists have drawn many parallels between the way our brains react to certain comfort foods and the way our brains react to listening to music. Music affects parts of the brain that trigger primitive reaction, emotional response, and the intellect. In a similar way, eating certain soothing foods can activate emotional associations, especially those stemming from childhood. This is what is termed the "food-mood connection."

Soups and stews are quintessential comfort foods, and in these hard economic times, we all need some comforting. The skyrocketing cost of food is a harsh reality, and it's one that is not going to go away. The era of "cheap food" that we knew and loved is gone forever, even if people in other countries still envy the fact that in the United States we spend less than 15 percent of our income on food.

The reasons for the rise in food costs are varied, and they're global rather than national or local. Even if the cost of a gallon of gas drops below that of a gallon of milk, the export tax placed on soybeans by the government of Argentina means that it costs more to feed American livestock.

Countries like India and China have been striving to increase the size of their middle class, and we hope all people in the world can reach a higher standard of living. But why is that important to us? You see the result when you look at the cost of everything in the meat case. Will it ever stop going up? Ground beef is more expensive today than a pot roast was last year.

That's where *$3 Soups and Stews,* and the other books in the *$3 Meals* series, and I can help. I want you to enjoy cooking, as well as relishing the results of your cooking. I want you to savor the flavors in your food, as well as appreciating the fact that you're feeding your family healthful food that's made with real ingredients.

Remember this simple equation: Cost = Convenience + Chemicals. That's a nasty trio, those "Three C's." And they're what you're combating when cooking the recipes in this book. You're cooking with fresh ingredients, not convenience products that are loaded with chemicals. Thus you're saving money and eating better food too.

As a general rule, it is safe to say that the more a food is handled by someone *other than you,* the more expensive it becomes. Carrot sticks are more expensive than whole carrots that take but seconds to peel and cut. Packages labeled "stew beef" are generally far more expensive, and of uncertain origin, when compared to the chuck roast sitting next to them.

And there's no reason to use these value-added products once you learn it just takes a few minutes in the kitchen to do it yourself—and come out with a superior product, too.

When you think soups and stews, you may also be thinking, "Who has time to cook those? I get home from work and need to have dinner on the table in minutes, not hours!" There are recipes in this book that can fulfill the need for speed, too.

While meat stews can take a few hours to reach that magical state of meltingly "fork tender," chicken stews and fish stews are all quick-cooking. Additionally, while some of the recipes for nutritious bean stews are made with dried beans that need time to soften, others are made with inexpensive canned beans and are on the table before the evening news is over.

Another way that the soup and stew recipes in this book will help your harried life is that they form an arsenal for your freezer of "dinner insurance." All of these foods freeze beautifully, so you can spend a drizzly Saturday afternoon making a few recipes in large batches, and then "nuke" them hot in the microwave oven in less time than it would take to have a nutritionally bankrupt pizza delivered.

These insurance meals take the stress out of your daily life, and they take your car out of the supermarket parking lot or drive-thru fast food line. And you'll have such variety in the meals you're putting on the table!

The recipes in *$3 Soups and Stews* are drawn from cuisines around the world. Your taste buds will be jetting away to many foreign capitals as you enjoy richly flavored foods that can all be made on your limited food budget.

But they are all comfortable and cozy recipes. Whether you grew up with them, or you're encountering them for the first time now, all these dishes are easy on your psyche. If the first time you cook them they don't feel like comfort food, try them again. The next time you eat them they'll seem like the old friend with whom you shared secrets on the front porch.

The late Laurie Colwin, whose prose as well as recipes I truly admire, wrote in her great book *Home Cooking* that "to feel safe and warm on a cold wet night, all you really need is soup." Just remember that comfort food got its name for a reason.

Happy cooking!

—Ellen Brown
Providence, Rhode Island

Acknowledgments

While writing a book is a solitary endeavor, its publication is always a team effort. My thanks go to:

Ed Claflin, my agent, for his constant support and good cheer.

Marry Norris, editorial director of lifestyle books, Globe Pequot Press, for her help in bringing this and other *$3 Meals* books to fruition.

Julie Marsh of Globe Pequot Press for shepherding this manuscript seamlessly through the editorial process, and Jessie Shiers for her eagle-eyed copyediting.

Diana Nuhn for her creative cover designs.

Sheryl Kober and Melissa Evarts for their work on the production of this book to make it as "user-friendly" as possible.

My many friends who shared their favorite recipes and culinary wisdom, especially to my dear sister, Nancy Dubler.

Tigger and Patches, my furry companions, who personally endorse all fish and seafood recipes.

Introduction

Soups and stews are part of all our childhoods, regardless of where those childhoods took place. If your parents are Hungarian, your first stew may have been a goulash made with heady paprika and finished with tart sour cream; the dish has been part of that nation's repertoire since the ninth century. Or what if your family came to the United States from Italy, as millions did in the nineteenth and twentieth centuries? Chances are you grew up eating thick and hearty minestrone, filled with vegetables, beans, and pasta.

Entree soups and stews are one-pot cooking raised to the finest level, as they have been since prehistoric times. The development of pottery about 10,000 years ago facilitated simmering foods in liquid, and some prehistoric peoples also used the shells of large tortoises and other animals.

The ancient Greek historian Herodotus says that in the eighth century B.C.E. the Scythians were already making stews, and the Book of Genesis states that Esau traded his inheritance to his twin brother, Jacob, for a bowl of lentil stew. We're still eating lentils all around the world, especially in the Middle East, and you'll find some great ways to prepare them in this book.

What the ancients knew is still true today about these two soft and comforting forms of cooking; soups and stews are inherently inexpensive and can stretch to feed a crowd. And we need that today, as the cost of food skyrockets.

Next to housing and auto expenses, food is our major annual expense, as it is around the world. The fact that Americans spend about a 15 percent chunk of disposable income on food still remains the envy of most people living in the industrialized world. Just across the border in Canada the figure is 18 percent, while in Mexico it is more than 25 percent. To put this into context, from January 1 to mid-February, all the money you make goes to your yearly food budget.

While the recipes in Chapter 3 are for "small soups" to serve as appetizers, the remaining recipes in *$3 Soups and Stews* are intended to be served as the entree itself. For the purposes of definition, I call a soup a dish that is served in a bowl with a spoon. A stew, on the other hand, while it can be served in a bowl, contains less liquid and can also be served on a plate; it's always accompanied by a knife and fork, but you can also offer a soupspoon alongside.

Soups and stews share many common traits. The two genres are cooked in liquid and contain many ingredients that provide both flavor and nourishment. In soups the pieces of food are usually smaller because no cutting should be required, and the broth—called a gravy or sauce when it's a stew—is usually thinner.

The recipes in this book are organized by dominant ingredient—vegetables, chicken, fish, and meats. The soup recipes to be served with a spoon are at the beginning of each chapter, and the stew recipes follow.

The foundation of *$3 Soups and Stews,* as well as the other books in the *$3 Meals* series, is all the tricks I've learned in professional kitchens—including my own catering kitchen. Professional cooks learn to minimize waste; wasted food translates to lower profit.

That means that the onion peels and celery leaves that you might be throwing into your compost bin or garbage can now become an asset because you'll freeze them to make stocks. And you'll know you have succeeded in waste-free cooking when, at the end of the week, there's nothing in the refrigerator to throw away! That's quite a feeling of empowerment, and along the way you've been eating like royalty on a peon's budget.

The goal of the *$3 Meals* series is an ambitious one; this small amount of money—less than the cost of a large fast food burger or a slice of gourmet pizza—is for your *whole meal!* That includes the greens for your tossed salad and the dressing with which it's tossed. It includes the pasta or rice you cook to enjoy all the gravy from a stew. And it includes a sweet treat for dessert. So unlike many books that promise cost-conscious cooking, this book means it!

In addition to eating wonderfully, you'll also be eating more healthfully. It may not be by accident that "convenience" and "chemical" start with the same letter. Chemicals are what convenience foods are all about; they are loaded up with them to increase their shelf life, both before and after being opened. The recipes in this book don't contain such unhealthy ingredients as trans fats and high fructose corn syrup that can be hidden in processed foods, too.

One of the rules of economical cooking is that the more processed a food is, the more expensive it is. These recipes are made with foods that are ingredients; at one time they grew from the earth, walked upon it, and swam in its waters. The most processing that has taken place is the milk of animals being transformed into natural cheeses. So when you're cooking from *$3 Soups and Stews,* you're satisfying your body as well as your budget.

There are a few ingredient compromises made to trim costs; however, these shortcuts trim preparation time, too. The books in this series are the first I've written for which I used bottled lemon and lime juice in recipe development rather than freshly squeezed juices from the fruits themselves; I discovered it took a bit more juice to achieve the flavor I was after, but with the escalated cost of citrus fruits this was a sacrifice that I chose to make.

The same is true with vegetables; many of these recipes call for cost-effective frozen vegetables rather than fresh. For vegetables such as the chopped spinach added to a soup or casserole or the peas added to many dishes, it really doesn't matter.

I've also limited the range of dried herbs and spices specified to a core group of less than a dozen. There's no need to purchase an expensive jar of anise seed or dried marjoram that you may never use again.

On the other hand, there are standards I will never bend. I truly believe that unsalted butter is so far superior to margarine that any minimal cost savings from using margarine is not worth the trade-down in flavor. Good quality Parmesan cheese, freshly grated when you need it, is another ingredient well worth the splurge. You use very little of it, because once grated it takes up far more volume than in a block, and its innate flavor is far superior.

The same is true for using fresh parsley, cilantro, and dill. While most herbs deliver flavor in their dried form, these leafy herbs do not. Luckily, they are used so often that they are inexpensive to buy and don't go to waste—especially with the tricks I'll teach you on how to freeze them.

Each recipe in the book is annotated with the number of servings; it's a range because soups and stews can stretch so easily. Other annotations are for the amount of "hands-on" time you will be spending slicing and dicing the ingredients. While economy is a bonus with soups and stews, they do take more time to prepare than seasoning a whole chicken to roast in the oven or tossing some burgers on the grill.

The last annotation is for the time it takes between turning on the lights in the kitchen and sitting down at the table to enjoy your meal. Depending on the food being prepared, this can be as little as 30 minutes or up to four hours. But during the time the food is cooking, you can be doing something else.

Interspersed with the recipes are some boxes containing nuggets of kitchen wisdom or some fun facts about cooking. I've been a cookbook author for more than two decades, and I want to share some tricks of the trade with you.

Chapter 1:

Saving Money at the Supermarket

Food is big business in America; from the producers of the raw ingredients or commodities to the processors who take it from them to the supermarkets that sell it to you, every step of the way someone is making money. The money they're making is ultimately coming out of your pocket; what you're going to learn in this chapter is how to keep more of that money for yourself.

As you can well imagine, as a cookbook author I spend a lot of time in supermarkets, as well as other venues—from picturesque farmers' markets to the food aisles of chain drug stores—that sell food. One thing is certain, every other customer I talk to is as interested as you are and I am in eating better on a limited food budget. Those are the strategies you'll learn in this chapter.

Think of plotting and planning your supermarket trips as if you were planning for a vacation. Your first step is to decide on your destination—what supermarket or other stores you'll use. After that, you buy some guidebooks (in this case the Sunday newspaper) and do other research online (like print out coupons), and then you start looking for the good deals to get you to where you want to go.

In this case, where you want to go is to treat yourself to a vacation, and the way you're going to afford it in these challenging economic times is by savvy shopping. At any given moment there are *billions* of dollars of grocery coupons in the world waiting to be redeemed. Those coupons add up to big savings at the grocery store. For some other savings you have to spend a few cents on a stamp to get a rebate from a company, but it's worth it.

In fact, in one week of following the tips in this chapter, you will have more than made up for the cost of this book—and then you'll have all the cost-busting recipes to pamper your palate for years to come.

Most of the tips are specific to food shopping; this *is* a cookbook. But there are also hints for saving money in other segments of your budget. It's all coming out of the same wallet.

I wish I could promise you a clear and uncluttered path. But every rule has an exception, as you'll see below. What you're now doing is turning shopping from a simple ritual to a complex task. But the results are worth the effort you'll be putting in.

TIME FOR MENTAL CALISTHENICS

Just as an athlete goes through mental preparation before a big game, getting yourself "psyched" to save money is the first step to accomplishing that goal. You've got to get into a frugal frame of mind. You're out to save money on your food budget, but not feel deprived. You're going to be eating the delicious dishes in this book.

Think about where your food budget goes other than the grocery store. The cost of a few "designer coffee" treats at the local coffee shop is equal to a few dinners at home. Couldn't you brew coffee and take it to work rather than spend $10 a week at the coffee cart? And those cans of soft drinks in the vending machine are four times the cost of bringing a can from home. But do you really need soft drinks at all? For mere pennies you can brew a few quarts of iced tea, which has delicious flavor without chemicals.

Planning ahead is important, too. Rather than springing for a chilled bottle of spring water because you're thirsty in the supermarket, keep a few empty plastic bottles in your car and fill one from the water fountain. That water is free.

Until frugality comes naturally, do what diet counselors suggest, and keep a log of every penny spent on food. Just as the "empty calories" add up, so do the "meaningless noshes."

Bringing your lunch to work does increase your weekly supermarket tab, but it accomplishes a few good goals. It adds funds to the bottom line of your total budget, and it allows you to control what you're eating—and when.

If you have a pressured job, chances are there are days that you end up eating from snack food vending machines or eating fast food at your desk. If you bring your lunch you know what it will be—even if you don't know when you'll be eating it.

Almost every office has both a refrigerator and a microwave oven, so lunch can frequently be a leftover from a dinner the night or two before, making the extra cost and cooking time minimal. And few foods reheat as well as soups and stews!

Frugality also extends to the grocery if you can reuse grocery bags or use your own bags. Many stores give you a few cents off your order for each new bag you *don't* use. Reuse of bags is clearly beneficial to the environment as less packaging ends up in landfills, plus it eventually puts a few dollars into your pocket.

PLAN *BEFORE* YOU SHOP

The most important step to cost-effective cooking is to decide logically and intelligently what you're going to cook for the week. That many sound simple, but if you're in the habit of deciding when you're leaving work at the end of the day, chances are you've ended up with a lot of frozen pizza or Chinese carry-out.

The first step is to "shop" in a place you know well; it's your own kitchen. Look and see what's still in the refrigerator, and how that food—which you've already purchased and perhaps also cooked—can be utilized. That's where many recipes in this book come into play. Some leftover cooked carrots? Just check the index of this book and see all the ways they could be put to use.

Now look and see what foods you have in the freezer. Part of savvy shopping is stocking up on foods when they're on sale; in fact, sales of freestanding freezers have grown by more than 10 percent during the past few years, while sales of all other major appliances have gone down. And with good reason—a freestanding freezer allows you to take advantage of sales. Foods like boneless, skinless chicken breasts—the time-crunched cook's best friend—go on sale frequently and are almost prohibitive in price when they're not on sale.

But preparing food for the freezer to ensure its future quality is important. Never freeze meats, poultry, or seafood in the supermarket wrapping alone. To guard against freezer burn, double wrap food in freezer paper or place it in a heavy resealable plastic bag. Mark the purchase date on raw food, and the date the food was frozen on cooked items, and use them within three months.

Most supermarkets offer a lower cost for buying larger quantities, and by freezing part of a package you can take advantage of that savings. Scan recipes and look at the amount of the particular meat specified; that's what size your packages destined for the freezer should be. A good investment is a kitchen scale to weigh portions, if you don't feel comfortable judging weight freestyle.

Keep a list taped to the front of your freezer. It should list contents and date when each package was frozen. Mark off foods as you take them out and add foods as you put them in.

Also, part of your strategy as a cook is actually to cook only a few nights a week or on one day of a weekend; that means when you're making recipes that can be doubled—like these soups and stews—you make larger batches and freeze a portion. Those meals are "dinner insurance" for nights you don't want to cook. Those are the nights that you previously would have brought in the bucket of chicken or the high-priced rotisserie chicken and spent far more money.

The other factor that enters into the initial planning is looking at your depletion list, and seeing what foods and other products need to be purchased. A jar of peanut butter or a bottle of dishwashing liquid might not factor into meal plans, but they do cost money—so they have to be factored into your budget. Some weeks you might not need many supplies, but it always seems to me that all of the cleaning supplies seem to deplete the same week.

Now you've got the "raw data" to look at the weekly sales circulars from your newspaper or delivered with your mail. Those sales, along with online research to accrue even more money-saving coupons, should form the core for your menu planning.

COUPON CLIPPING 101

It's part art, it's part science, and it all leads to more money in your wallet. Consider this portion of the chapter your Guerrilla Guide to Coupons. There's more to it than just clipping them. Of course, unless you clip them or glean them from other channels (see some ideas below), you can't save money. So that's where you're going to start—but, trust me, it's just the beginning.

Forget that image you have of the lady wearing the hairnet and the "sensible shoes" in line at the supermarket digging through what seems to be a bottomless pit of tiny pieces of paper looking for the right coupon for this or that. Clipping coupons—in case you haven't heard—is *cool.*

And it should be. At any given moment there are *billions of dollars* of coupons floating around out there, according to the folks at www.grocerycouponguide.com, one of the growing list of similar sites dedicated to helping you save money.

Not only is it becoming easier to access these savings, you're a Neanderthal if you don't. The fact that you're reading this book—and will be cooking from it—shows that you care about trimming the size of your grocery bill. So it's time to get with the program.

Coupon usage grew by a whopping 192 percent in the year between March 2008 and March 2009, according to Coupons.com, which has seen an increase of 25 percent per month in traffic to the site since the current recession began.

Even the Sunday newspaper (as long as it still exists) is a treasure trove of coupons. I found a $5 off coupon for a premium cat food my finicky cats like in a local paper, which cost 50 cents. It was worth it to buy four copies of the paper; I spent $2 but I then netted an $18 savings on the cat food.

The first decision you have to make is how you're going to organize your coupons. There are myriad ways and each has its fans. It's up to you to decide which is right for you, your family, and the way you shop:

- **Arrange the coupons by aisle in the supermarket** if you only shop in one store consistently.

- **Arrange them by category of product** (like cereals, cleaning supplies, dairy products, etc.) if you shop in many stores.

- **Arrange coupons alphabetically** if you have coupons that you use in various types of stores beyond the grocery store.

- **Arrange coupons by expiration date.** Coupons are only valid for a certain time period; it can be a few weeks or a few months. And part of the strategy of coupon clipping is to maximize the value, which frequently comes close to the expiration date. Some of the best coupons are those for "buy one, get one free." However, when the coupon first appears the item is at full price. But what about two weeks later when the item is on sale at your store? Then the "buy one, get one free" can mean you're actually getting four cans for the original retail price of one.

Sometimes coupons expire *before* their stated expiration date because retailers allot so many dollars per promotion. If, for example, a retailer is offering a free widget if you buy a widget holder, and the widgets run out, there's probably a way to justify turning you away. Read the fine print.

While you may just be becoming more aware of them, coupons are nothing new. They began in the late 1800s when Coca-Cola and Grape Nuts offered coupons to consumers. Currently more than 3,000 companies use coupons as part of their marketing plans, and shoppers save more than $5 billion a year by redeeming the coupons.

Storage systems for arranging coupons are as varied as methods of organizing them. I personally use envelopes, and I keep the stack held together with a low-tech paper clip. I've also seen people with whole wallets and tiny accordion binders dedicated to coupons. If you don't have a small child riding on the top of the cart, another alternative is to get a loose-leaf notebook with clear envelopes instead of pages.

LEARN THE LINGO

Coupons are printed on very small pieces of paper, and even with 20/20 vision or reading glasses, many people—including me—need to use a magnifying glass to read all the fine print. There are many legal phrases that have to be part of every coupon, too.

In the same way that baseball fans know that RBI means "runs batted in," coupon collectors know that WSL means "while supplies last." Here's a list of many abbreviations found on coupons:

AR. After rebate.

B1G1 or BOGO. Buy one, get one free.

CRT. Cash register receipt.

DC. Double coupon, which is a coupon the store—not the manufacturer—doubles in value.

DCRT. Dated cash register receipt, which proves you purchased the item during the right time period.

FAR. Free after rebate.

IP. Internet printed coupons.

ISO. In-store only.

IVC. Instant value coupon, which are the pull-offs found on products in the supermarket that are redeemed as you pay.

MIR. Mail-in rebate.

NED. No expiration date.

OAS. On any size, which means the coupon is good for any size package of that particular product.

OYNSO. On your next shopping order, which means that you must return to the same store; the coupon will not be good at another store.

POP. Proof of purchase, which are the little panels found on packages that you have to cut off and send in to receive a rebate.

WSL. While supplies last, which means you can't demand a "rain check" to use the coupon at a later date when the product is once again in stock.

BARGAIN SHOPPING 2.0

Every grocery store has weekly sales, and those foods are the place to start your planning for new purchases; that's how you're saving money beyond using coupons. And almost every town has competing supermarket chains that offer different products on sale. It's worth your time to shop in a few venues, because it will generate the most savings. That way you can also determine which chain offers the best store brands and purchase them while you're there for the weekly bargains. Here are other ways to save:

- **Shuffle those cards.** Even if I can't convince you to clip coupons, the least you can do for yourself to save money is to take the five minutes required to sign up for store loyalty cards; many national brands as well as store brands are on sale only when using the card. While the current system has you hand the card to the cashier at the checkout, that will be changing in the near future. Shopping carts will be equipped with card readers that will generate instant coupons according to your purchasing habits. I keep my stack of loyalty cards in the glove box of my car; that way they don't clutter my purse but I always have them when shopping.

- **"Junk mail" may contain more than junk.** Don't toss those Valpak and other coupon envelopes that arrive in the mail. Look through them carefully, and you'll find not only coupons for food products, but for many services, too.

- **Look for blanket discounts.** While it does take time to cull coupons, many supermarket chains send flyers in the mail that offer a set amount off the total, for example $10 off a total of $50. This is the easiest way to save money, and many national drugstore chains, such as CVS, do the same. Just remember to have a loyalty card for those stores to take advantage of the savings.

- **Spend a stamp to get a rebate.** Despite the current cost of a first-class postage stamp, sending in for rebates is still worth your trouble. Many large manufacturers are now sending out coupon books or cash vouchers usable in many stores to customers who mail in receipts demonstrating that they have purchased about $50 of products. For example, Procter & Gamble, the country's largest advertiser and the company for which the term "soap opera" was invented, is switching millions of dollars from the airwaves to these sorts of promotions.

- **Find bargains online.** It's difficult for me to list specific Web sites because they may be defunct by the time you're reading this book, but there are hundreds of dollars worth of savings to be culled by printing coupons from Web sites, and for high-end organic products, it's the only way to access coupons. Sites I use frequently are www.couponmom.com and www.coupons.com, and I also look for the coupon offers on such culinary sites as www.epicurious.com and www.foodnetwork.com. You will find coupons there, some tied to actual recipes. Also visit manufacturers' Web sites, which offer both coupons and redemption savings.

- **Find coupons in the store.** Look for those little machines projecting out from the shelves; they usually contain coupons that can be used instantly when you check out. Also, don't throw out your receipt until you've looked at it carefully. There are frequently coupons printed on the back. The cashier may also hand you other small slips of paper with your cash register receipt; most of them are coupons for future purchases of items you just bought. They may be from the same brand or they may be from a competing brand. Either way, they offer savings.

- **Stock up on cans.** Even if you live in a small apartment without a basement storage unit, it makes sense to stock up on canned goods when they're on sale. The answer is to use every spare inch of space. The same plastic containers that fit under your bed to hold out-of-season clothing can also become a pantry for canned goods.

- **Get a bargain buddy.** There's no question that supermarkets try to lure customers with "buy one, get one free" promotions, and sometimes one is all you really want. And those massive cases of paper towels at the warehouse clubs are also a good deal—if you have unlimited storage space. The answer? Find a bargain buddy with whom you can split large purchases. My friends and I also swap coupons we won't use for ones we will. Going back to my example of the cat food savings, there were dog food coupons on the same page, so I turned them over to a canine-owning friend.

PUSHING THE CART WITH PURPOSE

So it's a "new you" entering the supermarket. First of all, you have a list, and it's for more than a few days. And you're going to buy what's on your list. Here's the first rule: stick to that list. Never go shopping when you're hungry; that's when non-essential treats wind up in your basket.

Always go shopping alone; unwanted items end up in the cart to keep peace in the family. And—here's an idea that might seem counter-intuitive—go shopping when you're in a hurry. It's those occasions when you have the time to dawdle that the shortcakes end up coming home when all you really wanted were the strawberries.

But as promised, here are some exceptions to the rule of keeping to your list. You've got to be flexible enough to take advantage of some unexpected great sales. Next to frugality, flexibility is the key to saving money on groceries.

It's easy if the sale is a markdown on meat; you see the $2 off coupon and put it in the cart, with the intention of either cooking it that night or freezing it. All supermarkets mark down meat on the day before the expiration sticker. The meat is still perfectly fine, and should it turn out not to be, you can take it back for a refund. So go ahead and take advantage of the markdown.

Then you notice a small oval sticker with the word "Save." Is turkey breast at $1.09 a real bargain? You'll know it is if you keep track of prices and know that a few weeks ago it was $3.99 per pound.

You now have two options. Buy the off-list bargains and freeze them, or use them this week. In place of what? And what effect will that have on the rest of your list?

That's why I suggest freezing bargains, assuming you can absorb the extra cost on this week's grocery bill. If not, then look at what produce, shelf-stable, and dairy items on the list were tied to a protein you're now crossing off, and delete them too.

But meat isn't the only department of the supermarket that has "remainder bins." Look in produce, bakery, and grocery. I've gotten some perfectly ripe bananas with black spots—just the way they should be—for pennies a pound, while the ones that are bright yellow (and still tasteless) are five times the cost.

Most supermarkets are designed to funnel traffic first into the produce section—that is the last place you want to shop. Instead, begin with the proteins, since many items in other sections of your list relate to the entrees of the dinners you have planned. Once they are gathered, go through and get the shelf-stable items, then the dairy products (so they will not be in the cart for too long), and end with the produce. Using this method, the fragile produce is on the top of the basket, not crushed by the gallons of milk.

The last step is packing the groceries. If your store allows you the option of packing them yourself, place items stored together in the same bag. That way all of your produce can go directly into the refrigerator, and canned goods destined for the basement will be stored in one trip.

LEARNING THE ROPES

The well-informed shopper is the shopper who is saving money, and the information you need to make the best purchasing decision is right there on the supermarket shelves. It's the shelf tag that gives you the cost per unit of measurement. The units can be quarts for salad dressing, ounces for dry cereal, or pounds for canned goods. All you have to do is look carefully.

But you do have to make sure you're comparing apples to apples and oranges to oranges—or in this example, stocks to stocks. Some can be priced by the quart, while others are by the pound.

- **Check out store brands.** Store brands and generics have been improving in quality during the past few years, and according to *Consumer Reports,* buying them can save anywhere from 15 to 50 percent. Moving from a national brand to a store brand is a personal decision, and sometimes money is not the only factor. For example, I have used many store brands of chlorine bleach, and I have returned to Clorox time and again. But I find no difference between generic cornflakes and those from the market leaders. Store brands can also be less expensive than national brands on sale—and with coupons.

- **Compare prices within the store.** Many foods—such as cold cuts and cheeses—are sold in multiple areas of the store, so check out those alternate locations. Sliced ham may be less expensive in a cellophane package shelved with the refrigerated foods than at the deli counter.

- **Look high and low.** Manufacturers pay a premium price to shelve products at eye level, and you're paying for that placement when you're paying their prices. Look at the top and bottom shelves in aisles like cereal and canned goods. That's where you'll find the lower prices.

- **Buy the basics.** When is a bargain not a bargain? When you're paying for water or you're paying for a little labor. That's why even though a 15-ounce can of beans is less expensive than the same quantity of dried beans (approximately a pound), you're still better off buying the dried beans. One pound of dried beans makes the equivalent of four or five cans of beans. In the same way, a bar of Monterey Jack cheese is much less expensive per pound than a bag of grated Monterey Jack cheese. In addition to saving money, the freshly grated cheese will have more flavor because cheese loses flavor rapidly when grated. And pre-cut and pre-washed vegetables are truly exorbitant.

- **Watch the scanner.** I know it's tempting to catch up on pop culture by leafing through the tabloids at the checkout, but that's the last thing you should be doing. Watching the clerk scan your order usually saves you money. For example, make sure all the instant savings coupons are peeled off; this includes marked-down meats and coupons on boxes and bags. Then, make sure sale items are ringing up at the right price.

WASTE NOT, WANT NOT

We're now going to start listing exceptions to all the rules you just read, because a bargain isn't a bargain if you end up throwing some of it away. Remember that the goal is to waste nothing. Start by annotating your shopping list with quantities for the recipes you'll be cooking. That way you can begin to gauge when a bargain is a bargain. Here are other ways to buy only what you need:

- **Don't overbuy.** Sure, the large can of diced tomatoes costs less per pound than the smaller can. But what will you do with the remainder of the can if all you need is a small amount? The same is true for dairy products. A half-pint of heavy cream always costs much more per ounce than a quart, but if the remaining three cups of cream will end up in the sink in a few weeks, go with the smaller size.

- **Buy what you'll eat, not what you *should* eat.** If your family hates broccoli, the low sale cost doesn't matter; you'll end up throwing it away. We all think about healthful eating when we're in the supermarket, but if you know that the contents of your cart are good thoughts rather than realistic choices, you're wasting money.

- **Just because you have a coupon doesn't mean you should buy something.** We all love bargains, but if you're putting an item into your cart for the first time, you must decide if it's because you really want it or because you're getting $1.50 off its cost.

- **Sometimes bigger isn't better.** If you're shopping for snacks for a young child, look for the *small* apples rather than the giant ones. Most kids take a few bites and then toss the rest, so evaluate any purchases you're making by the pound.

- **Ring that bell!** You know the one; it's always in the meat department of the supermarket. It might take you a few extra minutes, but ask the real live human who will appear for *exactly* what you want; many of the recipes in *$3 Soups and Stews* specify less than the weight of packages you find in the meat case. Many supermarkets do not have personnel readily available in departments like the cheese counter, but if there are wedges of cheeses labeled and priced, then someone is in charge. It might be the deli department or the produce department, but find out who it is and ask for a small wedge of cheese if you can't find one that's cut to the correct size.

- **Check out the bulk bins.** Begin buying from the bulk bins for shelf-stable items, like various types of rice, beans, dried fruits, and nuts. Each of these departments has scales so you can weigh ingredients like dried mushrooms or pasta. If a recipe calls for a quantity rather than a weight, you can usually "eyeball" the quantity. If you're unsure of amounts, start by bringing a 1-cup measuring cup with you to the market. Empty the contents of the bin into the measuring cup rather than directly into the bag. One problem with bulk food bags is that they are difficult to store in the pantry; shelves were made for sturdier materials. Wash out plastic deli containers or even plastic containers that you bought containing yogurt or salsa. Use those for storage once the bulk bags arrive in the kitchen. Make sure you label your containers of bulk foods, both at the supermarket and when transferring the foods to other containers at home, so you know what they are, especially if you're buying similar foods. Arborio and basmati rice look very similar in a plastic bag, but they are totally different grains and shouldn't be substituted for each other.

- **Shop from the salad bar for tiny quantities.** There's no question that supermarkets charge a premium price for items in those chilled bins in the salad bar, but you get exactly what you need. When to shop there depends on the cost of the item in a larger quantity. At $4 per pound, you're still better off buying a 50-cent can of garbanzo beans, even if it means throwing some of them away. However, if you don't see how you're going to finish the $4 pint of cherry tomatoes, then spend $1 at the salad bar for the handful you need to garnish a salad.

SUPERMARKET ALTERNATIVES

All of the hints thus far in this chapter have been geared to pushing a cart around a supermarket. Here are some other ways to save money:

- **Shop at farmers' markets.** I admit it; I need a twelve-step program to help me cure my addiction to local farmers' markets. Shopping *al fresco* on warm summer days turns picking out fruits and vegetables into a truly sensual experience. Also, you buy only what you want. There are no bunches of carrots; there are individual carrots sold by the pound. The U.S. Department of Agriculture began publishing the *National Directory of Farmers' Markets* in 1994, and at that time the number was fewer than 2,000. That figure has now doubled. To find a farmers' market near you, go to www.ams.usda.gov/farmersmarkets. The first cousins of farmers' markets for small quantities of fruits are the sidewalk vendors in many cities. One great advantage to buying from them is that their fruit is always ripe and ready to eat or cook.

- **Shop at ethnic markets.** If you live in a rural area this may not be possible, but even moderately small cities have a range of ethnic markets, and that's where you should buy ingredients to cook those cuisines. All the Asian condiments used in *$3 Soups and Stews* are far less expensive at Asian markets than in the Asian aisle of your supermarket, and you can frequently find imported authentic brands instead of U.S. versions. Even small cities and many towns have ethnic enclaves, such as a "Little Italy"; many neighborhoods have access to grocery stores with great prices for ethnic ingredients and the fresh produce used to make the dishes, too.

- **Shop alternative stores.** Groceries aren't only at grocery stores; many "dollar stores" and other discount venues stock shelf-stable items. Also, every national drugstore chain—including CVS and Walgreens—carries grocery products and usually has great bargains each week. In the same way that food markets now carry much more than foods, drugstores stock thousands of items that have no connection to medicine. Those chains also have circulars in Sunday newspapers, so check them out—even if you're feeling very healthy.

- **Shop online.** In recent years it's become possible to do all your grocery shopping online through such services as Peapod and Fresh Direct. While there is frequently a delivery charge involved, for housebound people this is a true boon. If you really hate the thought of pushing the cart, you should explore it; it's impossible to make impulse buys. There are also a large number of online retailers for ethnic foods, dried herbs and spices, premium baking chocolate, and other shelf-stable items. Letting your cursor do the shopping for these items saves you time, and many online shops offer free shipping at certain times of the year.

So now that you're becoming a grocery guru, you can move on to find myriad ways to save money on your grocery bill while eating wonderfully. That's what *$3 Soups and Stews* and the other books in the *$3 Meals* series are all about.

Chapter 2:

Soup and Stew Secrets

I know there's more to a meal than the dish you're serving as the entree. That's why I give you suggestions with each recipe for dishes—be it a salad or vegetable—to serve with the soup and stew. And that's why you'll find recipes for all manner of breads from around the world in Chapter 8.

But what you'll find in this chapter are recipes to enhance your soup- and stew-making abilities, and useful information on how to make the best soups and stews. The foundations of all the recipes in this book are richly flavored, long-simmered homemade stocks, and that's where this chapter begins, too. Those all-important stocks are followed by recipes for various carbohydrates to go under all of these stews.

A good rule is that the closer a food is to its raw and natural state, the better it will be for you. Whole grains—including such grains as brown rice, barley, buckwheat groats, and bulgur—are complex carbohydrates, while foods like white flour and refined sugar are simple carbohydrates. You want the complex carbohydrates that are filled with fiber. These whole grains are also high in antioxidants that help build your immune system.

Carbohydrates are foods composed of some combination of starches, sugar, and fiber; they provide the body with the energy we need for all activities and they break down into glucose, a sugar our cells use as a universal source of energy. The problem with the refined (or "bad") carbs is that they digest so quickly that they can cause a dramatic elevation in blood sugar, which can lead to weight gain and even to diabetes.

The complex (or "good") carbs digest much more slowly. This keeps your blood sugar and insulin levels from rising and falling too quickly; you'll feel fuller both sooner and for longer.

While some of the stew recipes in *$3 Soups and Stews* contain a carbohydrate—such as potatoes or beans—many do not. Recipes for some interesting complex carbohydrates end this chapter.

BRAISING WITH BRAVADO

"Braising" is what we call the way stews are made; if turning a hunk of meat over an open flame is man's oldest form of cooking, then braising—which is simmering the meat gently in liquid—is a close second. There were pots placed in glowing embers to accomplish the task thousands of years ago. We tend to call it "stewing" when the meat is in small pieces and "braising" when the pieces are large, but it's all the same technique.

What's great to know is that the best cuts of food to braise are also the least expensive. It's like magic. Braising makes tough meat tender, and it will make tender meat tough. And tough meat is the least expensive meat.

Think of it this way. The more exercise muscles get, the stronger they are. Just as your leg muscles get more exercise than the muscles around your waist, so the legs of a cow or lamb, or a chicken, too, for that matter, get more exercise than the muscles around the loin area in the middle. There is more information on specific types of protein in the appropriate chapters of this book, but as a general guideline, look for the least expensive cuts of meat; those will be the best for braising.

Braising is accomplished by cooking the meat slowly, keeping it moist and covered over low heat for a long amount of time. This process breaks down the tough connective tissue in the meat to collagen. Through time, the moisture and heat build and the collagen dissolves into gelatin at a temperature of about 140°F.

Heat also contracts and coils the muscle fibers. Over time, these fibers expel moisture and the meat becomes dry. But—and here's the great part—after even more time, the fibers in the meat relax and absorb the melted fat and melted gelatin. As for the vegetables, braising breaks down the cellulose in them and stretches the starches, thus making the vegetables—regardless of how woody and hard they start out—as tender as the meats.

The meat that we eat is muscle, made up of muscle fibers and connective tissue. The muscle fibers are the long thin strands we can actually see and think of as meat. The connective tissue is the thin, translucent film that you sometimes ask the butcher to remove and that helps hold the bundles of muscle fiber together. Connective tissue is made up of mostly collagen, a very strong protein that breaks down if enough heat is applied to it.

THE BENEFITS OF BROWNING

For red meats like beef, browning is the initial step to a delicious dish; it's an optional step for poultry and pork, and it's totally unnecessary for fish and seafood. Browning actually gives foods better flavor.

Called the Maillard reaction, it was named for an early-twentieth-century chemist, Louis Camille Maillard, who discovered it. It's a chemical reaction that takes place on the surface of meats that creates flavor. The reaction takes place when food reaches 285°F, and that can only be done in a hot pan before food is cooked. Otherwise the temperature of the meat only reaches 212°F, which is the simmering temperature of the braising liquid.

Browning seals in juices, and it makes foods more visually appealing, too. Here are some tips for browning foods to be braised:

- **Dry food well.** Moisture causes splatters, which messes up the stove and can burn the cook.
- **Preheat the pan.** You have to wait until the fat is very hot, or the food will not brown.
- **Don't crowd the pan.** For food to brown it needs room for the steam that's created to escape.
- **Preheat the broiler well if using that method.** All meats *not* coated with flour can be browned under the broiler as well as in a skillet. (Flour needs the fat in the pan to cook it properly.) But you want to preheat the broiler for at least 10 or 15 minutes to create the brown crust.

OTHER TIPS FOR TRIUMPHS

While browning meats is the most important technique you need to create a sensational stew, there are other tricks to maximize the flavor of your results. These are all very easy and can be transferred to recipes you make other than the ones in this book.

Always keep in mind that braising food is one of the easiest cooking methods to produce pleasing results; it's not brain surgery. But try these ideas to make your dishes even better:

- **Use the right pan.** While pots and pans can be expensive, they last for a lifetime, as do good knives. That makes it worth the investment in a heavy Dutch oven for making stews. It should have thick walls and a lid that fits tightly, and it should be able to go into the oven, so the handles must also be metal. It can double as a stockpot or a saucepan, too.

- **Add ingredients in the order specified.** What you're after is to reach the finish line—when a soup or stew has completed cooking—with all the individual ingredients cooked to the proper degree to make them tender without falling apart. That's why foods are added during the cooking process and shouldn't be added prior to the time specified.

- **Easy does it on the temperature.** When braising, the method is most effective if the food is cooked in liquid that is merely simmering. That's why the oven is set for 350°F for meat stews and low heat is used if cooking on top of the stove. Increasing the temperature of the oven actually retards the meat from becoming tender.

- **Reduce the juices for more intense flavor.** If your ingredients are tender, but you think the resulting gravy lacks flavor, it may be because not enough water has evaporated. In cooking, this process is called reduction, and—like a person losing weight—a sauce loses water. What you have to do is strain the solids out of the liquid, and then cook the liquid, uncovered, over medium-high heat until it reaches the consistency and flavor you want.

- **Don't season food until you're ready to serve it.** A corollary to reducing food is that if you've added salt and pepper prior to reducing, you may find your sauce over-seasoned.

- **If coating food with flour, make sure it is well browned.** It's important to cook the proteins that are in flour. That's why the butter and flour are cooked slowly before making a cream sauce or creamed soup, and that's why meats coated in flour are browned before adding liquid. Otherwise you run the risk of sauces tasting "pasty." Remember that white paste you used in elementary school?

- **Remove as much fat as you can after cooking.** If you've cooked a soup or stew in advance and refrigerated it, then removing the fat prior to reheating it is very easy. You merely remove and discard the layer from the top of the container, because it will have solidified once chilled. If serving the dish right after it's done cooking, tilt the pot slightly; put one side on a few pot holders or a trivet to elevate it. Then use a soup ladle to remove the fat, which will form a puddle on the top of the lower side of the pot.

TAKING IT SLOW

There's an entire book in the *$3 Meals* series devoted to the wonders of cooking in the slow cooker, and if you like the recipes in this book, then *$3 Slow-Cooked Meals: Delicious, Low-Cost Dishes from Both Your Slow Cooker and Stove* would be a good addition to your cookbook collection.

While the recipes in this book are not devised for the slow cooker, many of the stews could be cooked in that popular appliance. Not all dishes can be easily converted to slow-cooked dishes. Even if a dish calls for liquid, if it's supposed to be cooked or baked uncovered, chances are it will not be successfully transformed to a slow cooker recipe, because the food will not brown and the liquid will not evaporate.

But if a dish is cooked covered in a conventional oven or simmered covered over low heat on top of the stove, it can be cooked in a slow cooker—as long as the quantity of the recipe is appropriate.

A huge batch of stew that will fill the insert more than two-thirds full or a small amount of sauce that only covers the bottom of the insert by a few inches is not a good candidate. If this is the case, fiddle with the batch size to make it appropriate for the slow cooker.

Here are some general guidelines:

- Quadruple the time from conventional cooking to cooking on Low, and at least double it for cooking on High.

- Most any meat or poultry stew or roast takes 8 to 12 hours on Low and 4 to 6 hours on High.

- Chicken dishes cook more rapidly. Count on 6 to 8 hours on Low and 3 to 4 hours on High.

- Cut back on the amount of liquid used in stews and other braised dishes; the amount will depend on the recipe. Unlike cooking on the stove or in the oven, there is little to no evaporation when cooking in the slow cooker. If the food isn't totally covered with liquid when you start to cook, don't worry. Ingredients like meat, chicken, and many vegetables give off their own juices as they cook.

- For soups, cut back on the liquid by ¼ if the soup is supposed to simmer uncovered, and cut back by a few cups if the soup is simmered covered. Even when covered, a soup that is simmering on the stove has more evaporation than one cooked in the slow cooker.

- Add tender vegetables like tomatoes for only the last 45 minutes of cooking time.

STOCKING UP

These are the four most important recipes you'll find in this book; they form the foundation for all soups and stews. Even beyond soup and stew recipes that call for a lot of stock, this category of easily prepared food is found in almost all cooking.

It's the long-simmered homemade stocks that add the depth of flavor to the soups and sauces enjoyed at fine restaurants. Classically trained chefs have known for centuries what you're about to learn in this chapter—making stocks is as hard as boiling water and, if you're judicious and save bits and pieces destined for the garbage when prepping foods to be cooked, they're almost free.

Those onion and carrot peels, the bottom of celery ribs, and the stems from which you've stripped the leaves of fresh parsley are all used to flavor stocks. If you take the time to bone your own chicken breasts or cut up your own beef stew meat from a roast—which I encourage you to do and tell you how to do in the appropriate chapters—then you have everything you need to make stock.

Perhaps you never considered commercial stocks—many of which are loaded with sodium—to be a "convenience food." But that's what they are, and you'll start to experience a significant savings when you begin making them yourself. You can't save money by making a quart of milk in your own kitchen, but you can make stock!

Cans and cartons of stocks are priced in many supermarkets in a way to confuse you; some are calculated by the pound while others are by the ounce. Looking at a range of costs as well as flavors at a recent taste testing, a generic stock that tasted like salted water with some chemical chicken flavor was still a whopping $2 per quart, while one that actually had some flavor was almost $5 per quart.

Chicken Stock

This is the most important stock, because it's used for pork and vegetable dishes as well as recipes with poultry.

Yield: 4 quarts | **Active time:** 10 minutes | **Start to finish:** 4 hours

6 quarts water
5 pounds chicken bones, skin, and trimmings (including giblets)
4 celery ribs, rinsed and cut into thick slices
2 onions, trimmed and quartered (but not peeled)
2 carrots, trimmed, scrubbed, and cut into thick slices
2 tablespoons whole black peppercorns
6 garlic cloves, peeled
4 sprigs fresh parsley
1 teaspoon dried thyme
2 bay leaves

1. Place water and chicken in a large stockpot, and bring to a boil over high heat. Reduce the heat to low, and skim off foam that rises during the first 10–15 minutes of simmering. Simmer stock, uncovered, for 1 hour, then add celery, onions, carrots, peppercorns, garlic, parsley, thyme, and bay leaves. Simmer for 2½ hours.
2. Strain stock through a fine-meshed sieve, pushing with the back of a spoon to extract as much liquid as possible. Discard solids, spoon stock into smaller containers, and refrigerate. Remove and discard fat from surface of stock, then transfer stock to a variety of container sizes.

Note: The stock can be refrigerated and used within 3 days, or it can be frozen for up to 6 months.

Variation:

- For turkey stock, use an equal amount of turkey giblets and necks in place of chicken pieces.

> The giblets—the neck, heart, and gizzard—are what's in that little bag inside a whole chicken that you probably toss. Save them all for stock. But freeze the chicken liver separately. Livers cannot be used in stock, but once you've got enough of them, you can make a pâté or sauté the livers for dinner.

Beef Stock

While beef stock is not specified as often as chicken stock in recipes, it is the backbone to certain soups and the gravy for stews and roasts.

Yield: 2 quarts | **Active time:** 15 minutes | **Start to finish:** 3½ hours

2 pounds beef trimmings (bones, fat) or inexpensive beef shank
3 quarts water
1 carrot, trimmed, scrubbed, and cut into thick slices
1 medium onion, peeled and sliced
1 celery rib, rinsed, trimmed, and sliced
1 tablespoon whole black peppercorns
3 sprigs fresh parsley
1 teaspoon dried thyme
2 garlic cloves, peeled
2 bay leaves

1. Preheat the oven broiler, and line a broiler pan with heavy-duty aluminum foil. Broil beef for 3 minutes per side, or until browned. Transfer beef to a large stockpot, and add water. Bring to a boil over high heat. Reduce the heat to low, and skim off foam that rises during the first 10–15 minutes of simmering. Simmer for 1 hour, uncovered, then add carrot, onion, celery, peppercorns, parsley, thyme, garlic, and bay leaves. Simmer for 3 hours.
2. Strain stock through a fine-meshed sieve, pushing with the back of a spoon to extract as much liquid as possible. Discard solids, and spoon stock into smaller containers. Refrigerate; remove and discard fat from surface of stock.

Note: The stock can be refrigerated and used within 3 days, or it can be frozen for up to 6 months.

Variation:

- Should you find some inexpensive veal bones on sale—the one cut that can sometimes be found is breast of veal—then feel free to use them.

Vegetable Stock

You may think it's not necessary to use vegetable stock if making a vegetarian dish that includes the same vegetables, but that's not the case. Using stock creates a much more richly flavored dish that can't be replicated by increasing the quantity of vegetables cooked in it.

Yield: 2 quarts | **Active time:** 10 minutes | **Start to finish:** 1¼ hours

2 quarts water
2 carrots, trimmed, scrubbed, and thinly sliced
2 celery ribs, rinsed, trimmed, and sliced
2 leeks, white part only, trimmed, rinsed, and thinly sliced
1 small onion, peeled and thinly sliced
1 tablespoon whole black peppercorns
3 sprigs fresh parsley
1 teaspoon dried thyme
2 garlic cloves, peeled
1 bay leaf

1. Pour water into a stockpot, and add carrots, celery, leeks, onion, peppercorns, parsley, thyme, garlic, and bay leaf. Bring to a boil over high heat, then reduce the heat to low and simmer stock, uncovered, for 1 hour.
2. Strain stock through a fine-meshed sieve, pushing with the back of a spoon to extract as much liquid as possible. Discard solids, and allow stock to cool to room temperature. Spoon stock into smaller containers, and refrigerate.

Note: The stock can be refrigerated and used within 3 days, or it can be frozen for up to 6 months.

Variation:

- Substitute tarragon for the thyme, or substitute scallion tops for the leeks.

Seafood Stock

Seafood stock is a great reason to make friends with the head of the fish department of your supermarket. You can arrange in advance to have lobster bodies set aside for purchase at minimal cost if the store cooks lobster meat. The same is true with fish bones, if a store actually fillets the fish on site.

Yield: 2 quarts | **Active time:** 15 minutes | **Start to finish:** 1¾ hours

- 3 lobster bodies (whole lobsters from which the tail and claw meat has been removed) or shells from 3 pounds raw shrimp
- 3 quarts water
- 1 cup dry white wine
- 1 carrot, trimmed, scrubbed, and cut into 1-inch chunks
- 1 medium onion, peeled and sliced
- 1 celery rib, rinsed, trimmed, and sliced
- 1 tablespoon whole black peppercorns
- 3 sprigs fresh parsley
- 1 teaspoon dried thyme
- 2 garlic cloves, peeled
- 1 bay leaf

1. If using lobster shells, pull top shell off 1 lobster body. Scrape off and discard feathery gills, then break body into small pieces. Place pieces in the stockpot, and repeat with remaining lobster bodies. If using shrimp shells, rinse and place in the stockpot.
2. Add water, wine, carrot, onion, celery, peppercorns, parsley, thyme, garlic, and bay leaf. Bring to a boil over high heat, then reduce the heat to low and simmer stock, uncovered, for 1½ hours.
3. Strain stock through a fine-meshed sieve, pushing with the back of a spoon to extract as much liquid as possible. Discard solids, and allow stock to cool to room temperature. Spoon stock into smaller containers, and refrigerate.

Note: The stock can be refrigerated and used within 3 days, or it can be frozen for up to 6 months.

Variation:

- Substitute 2 pounds bones and skin from firm-fleshed white fish such as halibut, cod, or sole for the lobster bodies.

FROM CAULDRON TO CASSEROLE

Stew on top of a serving of an appropriate carbohydrate is always appealing. But it's really quite easy to transform almost any stew into either a crust-topped potpie or a potato-topped variation on traditional English shepherd's pie for a change of pace.

For both forms, the stew should be totally cooked in advance, and then placed hot in a 9 x 13-inch baking pan. For a potpie, once the crust is in place as described below, bake it at 375°F for 30–40 minutes, or until the crust is golden brown. For a potato-topped pie, bake the dish at 400°F for 15–20 minutes, or until the potatoes are lightly browned.

Basic Piecrust

Piecrust is essentially flour and fat, mixed with a little salt and water. Once you've made it a few times, you'll see how easy it is to make anything from potpies to traditional fruit pies and hand-held treats like empanadas.

Yield: Crust for 1 (9 x 13-inch) pie | **Active time:** 15 minutes | **Start to finish:** 15 minutes

1½ cups all-purpose flour
½ teaspoon salt
10 tablespoons (1¼ sticks) unsalted butter
4–5 tablespoons ice water

1. Combine flour and salt in a medium mixing bowl. Cut butter into cubes the size of lima beans, and cut into flour using a pastry blender, two knives, or your fingertips until mixture forms pea-sized chunks. This can also be done in a food processor fitted with the steel blade using on-and-off pulsing.
2. Sprinkle mixture with water, 1 tablespoon at a time. Toss lightly with fork until dough will form a ball. If using a food processor, process until mixture holds together when pressed between two fingers; if it is processed until it forms a ball, too much water has been added.
3. Form dough into a "pancake." Flour pancake lightly on both sides, and, if time permits, refrigerate dough before rolling it to allow more even distribution of the moisture.
4. Roll dough between 2 sheets of waxed paper into an 11 x 15-inch rectangle. Invert dough onto the top of the 9 x 13-inch baking pan on

top of hot stew. Attach crust to the edges of the pan by pressing with your finger to crimp pastry. Cut 6 (1-inch) vents into crust to allow steam to escape.

Note: The crust can be prepared up to 3 days in advance and refrigerated, tightly covered. Also, both dough "pancakes" and rolled-out sheets can be frozen for up to 3 months.

Variations:

- To create a fluted edge: Trim the pastry ½ inch beyond the edge of the pan, and fold under to make a plump pastry edge. Place your index finger on the inside of the pastry edge, thumb and middle finger on the outside. Pinch the pastry into V-shapes, and repeat the pinching to sharpen the design.
- For a shiny crust: Blend 1 egg yolk with 1 tablespoon milk or water. Brush over the top of the pie before cutting steam vents and baking.

Cheese and Potato Topping for Pies

While shepherd's pie, a classic of English cookery, is a unique dish, I use the concept of topping a stew with mashed potatoes for many dishes. I really like the addition of cheese, too.

Yield: Topping for 1 (9 x 13-inch) pie | **Active time:** 10 minutes | **Start to finish:** 25 minutes

1½ pounds redskin potatoes, scrubbed and cut into 1-inch dice
⅓ cup heavy cream
2 tablespoons unsalted butter
1 cup grated sharp cheddar cheese
Salt and freshly ground black pepper to taste

1. Place potatoes in a saucepan of salted water, and bring to a boil over high heat. Reduce the heat to medium and boil potatoes, uncovered, for 12–15 minutes, or until soft. Drain potatoes in a colander.
2. Heat cream, butter, and cheese in the saucepan over medium heat until cheese melts, stirring occasionally. Return potatoes to saucepan, and mash well with a potato masher. Season to taste with salt and pepper.
3. Spread an even layer of potato on top of hot stew by evenly spacing dollops on top of stew and then spreading them with a rubber spatula.

Note: The potato topping can be made up to 2 days in advance and refrigerated, tightly covered. Add 5–7 minutes to the baking time if potatoes are chilled.

Variations:

- Substitute Swiss cheese for the cheddar cheese.
- Add 2 tablespoons chopped fresh parsley and 1 teaspoon herbes de Provence to the potatoes.

DRESSING UP YOUR DISHES

One aspect many cooks perceive as a downside of serving soups and stews as entrees is that most food is soft and has a uniform texture when it finishes cooking. Soups and stews also have a uniform overall coloration when compared to meals composed of different recipes.

Here are some easy and inexpensive garnishes to create some visual fireworks when they appear on the table:

- Instead of adding cheese to a dish for the last part of the cooking time, sprinkle it on top of the food right before you serve it. This is especially good with hard cheeses like Parmesan or cheeses that crumble easily like feta or blue.

- For an unexpected crunch, add toasted croutons to the tops of stews and soups before serving.

- Sprigs of fresh herbs used while cooking the dishes add color.

- Toast nuts like slivered almonds or chopped walnuts in a 350°F oven for 5 minutes and sprinkle on stews before serving.

- Crumbled bacon is a good garnish for pork stews and hearty soups.

Basic Croutons

Crunchy bits of toast on top of a soup or stew, as well as on a salad, add textural variety. They are also a snap to make with stale bread. While some recipes call for sautéing them on top of the stove, I find it is much easier to bake them.

Yield: 3 cups | **Active time:** 10 minutes | **Start to finish:** 20 minutes

3 cups (½-inch) cubes French or Italian bread
⅓ cup olive oil
Salt and freshly ground black pepper to taste

1. Preheat the oven to 375°F, and line a baking pan with aluminum foil.
2. Place bread cubes in the baking pan, drizzle bread with olive oil, and sprinkle with salt and pepper. Toss cubes to coat evenly.
3. Bake cubes for a total of 10 minutes, or until brown and crunchy, turning them with a spatula after 5 minutes. Remove the pan from the oven, and allow cubes to come to room temperature. Store in an airtight container or resealable plastic bag at room temperature.

Note: The croutons can be prepared up to 1 week in advance and kept at room temperature in an airtight container.

Variations:

- Press 2 garlic cloves through a garlic press, and stir the garlic into the oil.
- Rather than using French bread, substitute herb bread, olive bread, or multigrain bread.
- Toss croutons with 1 tablespoon Italian seasoning or herbes de Provence before baking.
- Toss croutons with 3 tablespoons freshly grated Parmesan cheese before baking.

SOPPING UP THE SAUCE

Because stews are customarily served with knives and forks rather than exclusively with spoons, it's also customary to have some sort of plain food underneath the stew so you can enjoy every drop of the richly flavored sauce. It can be as simple as some pasta, rice, or buttered egg noodles. It can also be a slice of thick toast; untoasted bread is not recommended, however, because it falls apart too easily and is just mushy.

But there are other options, and some of them add healthful grains to your diet, too. Those are the recipes you'll find in this section.

Great Mashed Potatoes

I never met a potato I didn't like, and devising a recipe for what I considered to be the perfect mashed potato has been a quest of mine for decades. I like potatoes a bit lumpy, but if you want them smooth, push them through a potato ricer or a food mill. Never use a food processor or an electric mixer to make mashed potatoes; you'll end up with glue.

Yield: 4–6 servings | **Active time:** 15 minutes | **Start to finish:** 35 minutes

2 pounds Yukon Gold potatoes, peeled and cut into 1-inch cubes
6 cups cold water
2 teaspoons salt
2/3 cup half-and-half or whole milk
4 tablespoons (1/2 stick) unsalted butter
Freshly ground black pepper to taste

1. Combine potatoes, water, and salt in a 3-quart saucepan, and bring to a boil over high heat. Reduce the heat to medium, and cook potatoes, partially covered, for 10–15 minutes, or until very tender.
2. Drain potatoes in a colander, shaking the colander over the sink. Return potatoes to the pan. Cook over medium heat for 2 minutes, shaking the pan frequently. Transfer potatoes to a mixing bowl.
3. Heat half-and-half and butter in the saucepan until butter is melted. Pour mixture over potatoes, and mash with a potato masher until desired consistency is reached. Season to taste with salt and pepper, and serve immediately.

Note: The dish can be prepared up to 1 day in advance and refrigerated, tightly covered. Reheat it, covered, in a 350°F oven for 20–25 minutes, or until hot.

Variations:

- Puree ¼ cup roasted garlic with the half-and-half for roasted garlic mashed potatoes.
- Substitute olive oil for the butter.
- Substitute 1 (8-ounce) package cream cheese, softened, for the half-and-half.
- Reduce the butter to 2 tablespoons and add ¾ cup grated cheddar or Swiss cheese.

> Too many mashed potatoes is never a problem in my house. But if you do have more than you need, turn them into potato cakes—either as a side dish or as an entree with cooked ham or chicken added.

Creamy Polenta

Cooking polenta—basically a cornmeal mush—used to demand that the cook had great biceps; it needed almost constant stirring for a long period of time. This method, however, cooks the polenta covered, so stirring is reduced.

Yield: 4–6 servings | **Active time:** 10 minutes | **Start to finish:** 45 minutes

3 cups water
1 cup whole milk
1 teaspoon salt
1 cup polenta
2 tablespoons unsalted butter, cut into small bits
Freshly ground black pepper to taste

1. Bring water, milk, and salt to a boil in a 3-quart saucepan over high heat. Add polenta in a thin stream, whisking so no lumps form.
2. Reduce the heat to medium, and continue to whisk for 2 minutes. Cover the pan, reduce the heat to the lowest setting, and stir with a heavy spoon every 8–10 minutes for 30 seconds, or until polenta is smooth again. Continue to cook for 30 minutes.
3. Remove the pan from the heat, and stir in butter. Season to taste with salt and pepper, and serve immediately.

Note: The dish can be prepared up to 20 minutes in advance. If holding it for longer than that, add additional milk and butter to create a creamy consistency again.

Variations:

- Substitute chicken stock or vegetable stock for the water.
- Add 2 tablespoons chopped fresh parsley and ½ teaspoon Italian seasoning to the water.
- Along with the butter, add ½–¾ cup grated cheese: whole-milk mozzarella, a combination of whole-milk mozzarella and fresh Parmesan, or Swiss.

- For crispy polenta, make the recipe above, and pack it into a well-greased 9 x 5 x 3-inch loaf pan. Chill well. Unmold the loaf, and cut into 1-inch slices. Cut each slice into 2 triangles. Heat 3 tablespoons olive oil in a large skillet over medium-high heat. Add polenta triangles, and cook for 2–3 minutes per side, or until browned and crisp, turning triangles gently with a spatula.

Polenta is a coarse yellow cornmeal. If you want to use regular yellow cornmeal for this dish, it will cook in 20 minutes.

Bulgur Pilaf

Bulgur is whole kernels of wheat that have been washed, steamed, hulled, and then cracked into various granulations. It is similar to cracked wheat, but it is precooked so it has a deeper gold color and a toastier flavor.

Yield: 4–6 servings | **Active time:** 15 minutes | **Start to finish:** 35 minutes

3 tablespoons olive oil
1 medium onion, peeled and chopped
1½ cups bulgur
2¼ cups water
Salt and freshly ground black pepper to taste

1. Heat oil in a saucepan over medium-high heat. Add onion, and cook, stirring frequently, for 5–8 minutes, or until onion is lightly browned.
2. Add bulgur and water, and season to taste with salt and pepper. Bring to a boil over high heat, stirring occasionally. Reduce the heat to low, cover the pan, and cook for 12–15 minutes, or until liquid is absorbed. Remove the pan from the heat, and allow bulgur to sit, covered, for 5 minutes. Fluff bulgur with a fork, adjust seasoning, and serve immediately.

Note: The dish can be prepared up to 2 days in advance and refrigerated, tightly covered. Reheat it, covered, in a 350°F oven for 20–25 minutes, or until hot.

Variations:

- To use bulgur under a stew that contains dried fruit, add ½ teaspoon ground cinnamon to the water.
- To go under a Middle Eastern stew, sauté 2 garlic cloves, peeled and minced, along with the onions, and add 1 teaspoon ground cumin and ½ teaspoon ground coriander to the water.

Bulgur is one of the grains that add a good serving of complex carbohydrates to your diet. To learn more about healthy eating as advised in the 2005 version of the Dietary Guidelines for Americans from the U.S. Department of Agriculture, visit www.mypyramid.gov.

Buckwheat Groats (Kasha)

Buckwheat groats are important in Eastern European cooking, and I love their nutty flavor under all hearty stews. The nuttiness is intensified by coating the grains with egg and toasting them before cooking.

Yield: 4–6 servings | **Active time:** 15 minutes | **Start to finish:** 30 minutes

1½ cups roasted buckwheat groats
2 large eggs, lightly beaten
3 cups boiling water
2 tablespoons olive oil
Salt and freshly ground black pepper to taste

1. Combine buckwheat groats and eggs in a dry 4-quart saucepan, and stir well to coat grains. Cook over medium heat, stirring constantly, for 2 minutes, or until grains separate.
2. Add water, oil, salt, and pepper. Reduce the heat to low, cover the pan, and cook for 10–12 minutes, or until water is almost absorbed. Remove the pan from the heat, and let stand, covered, for 10 minutes.
3. Season to taste with salt and pepper, and fluff with a fork before serving.

Note: The dish can be prepared up to 2 days in advance and refrigerated, tightly covered. Reheat it, covered, in a 350°F oven for 20–25 minutes, or until hot.

Variation:

- The traditional Eastern European variation called *kasha varnishkes* is a combination of buckwheat groats and cooked bow-tie pasta with some sautéed onions.

Basic Crostini

"Crostini" is a fancy word for thick toast, and they're always perfect for soaking up the juices of any stew.

Yield: 4–6 servings | **Active time:** 5 minutes | **Start to finish:** 20 minutes

8–12 (1-inch) slices French or Italian bread
½ cup olive oil
Salt and freshly ground black pepper to taste

1. Preheat the oven to 375°F, and cover a baking sheet with heavy-duty aluminum foil.
2. Brush bread slices with olive oil, and sprinkle with salt and pepper. Arrange slices on the baking sheet. Bake for 12–15 minutes, or until golden.

Note: The crostini can be made up to 3 days in advance and kept at room temperature in an airtight container.

Variations:

- Substitute olive bread, herb bread, or whole wheat bread for the white bread.
- Rub bread slices with a cut garlic clove before baking.
- Sprinkle slices with freshly grated Parmesan cheese before baking.

> If you made too many crostini, just break them apart into small squares and use them as croutons for soups or salads.

FROM PADDY TO PAN

All 2,500 species of rice, the world's most popular grain, trace their lineage to India. When rice comes from the field, it is termed "paddy rice," and it must have the non-edible hull removed before it can be eaten.

Brown rice—a long-time staple of the vegetarian diet and now gaining favor due to its higher fiber content—is whole or broken kernels of rice from which only the hull has been removed. For white rice, the grains are rubbed together to remove the natural bran.

Most species of rice are cooked in the same way—gently while covered in some sort of liquid with a little salt and fat (which can be butter or oil). Once the liquid comes to a boil, the pot should be covered and not stirred. Stirring releases the starch from the grains and makes the rice sticky. All rice should be fluffed with a fork before being served. Here are the main ways to cook it:

- **On top of the stove.** Simmer rice for 15–25 minutes.
- **In the oven.** Start with the liquid boiling, and bake the rice for 30–45 minutes at 350°F.
- **Brown rice.** A two-stage method produces brown rice that is cooked through and fluffy. Bring 2 quarts of water to a boil with 1 teaspoon salt and 2 tablespoons oil. Add 1 cup of brown rice and boil, uncovered, for 30 minutes. Drain the rice, and then steam it in a colander over boiling water for 5–10 minutes.

Chapter 3:
Small Soups for $1

There's an old Spanish proverb: "Of soup and love, the first is best." I frequently begin meals with a small soup, regardless of what follows. It shows caring, and it's my favorite way to begin a meal. It's these little soups—with their little price tags—that you'll find in this chapter.

In summer, chilled soups cool the spirit as effectively as steaming bowls of soup take the chill from even the most blizzardy winter day. Another advantage to beginning a meal with soup is that it's filling, so the stomach begins to feel satisfied instantly.

The pleasure of soup shouldn't be limited to seated meals. I fill thermos jugs with soups for picnics. Or take it to the office for lunch; almost every office now has a microwave oven to reheat soups to be eaten hot and a refrigerator to keep chilled soups cold.

The majority of the soup recipes in this chapter are quick and easy purees. In my experience there's a finite amount of time that most cooks will spend on any meal, even a formal party. I would rather put the effort into the main course and have the first course be memorable for its careful blending of flavors, not time-consuming preparation.

These recipes are written for appetizer portions, but some of them are thick and hearty enough to serve as an entree. If served as an entree, the soups will feed four to six people.

The vegetable soups are all written for chicken stock, but any of them can be made with vegetable stock as well. The chicken stock gives them a slightly richer flavor, and the calorie count will remain the same.

I don't give serving suggestions with the recipes in this chapter because these are appetizers rather than entree portions.

DEALING WITH DAIRY

Most of the recipes in this chapter are for simple creamed soups; they are thickened either with a bit of flour before the stock is added, or with some of the vegetables pureed. You'll notice that the dairy product is added after the vegetables have cooked in the stock. The reason for that is that all dairy products have the tendency to scorch, which ruins the flavor of the soup as well as its texture.

You'll also notice that I usually give the option of half-and-half or whole milk as the dairy product. When I was first learning to cook in the early 1960s, cream soups were never written with an ingredient other than heavy cream, and in many classic French cookbooks the recipes still call for cream. But I don't find that the extra saturated fat and calories brought to a soup by cream are that appealing today; our palates have become accustomed to eating lighter food. In addition, heavy cream is much more expensive than half-and-half because it contains more of the prized butterfat—that's what's removed and sold separately as butter.

On the other hand, two recipes cry out for the richness of heavy cream. In these cases, I think you'll be disappointed if you use a lighter product.

While whole milk is an option, I strongly warn you against using any dairy product with less fat, such as 2 percent milk or skim milk. Even if you're accustomed to drinking these reduced-fat products or using them in your coffee, I think you'll find that the soups taste watery if made with them.

PERSONALIZING THE PROCEDURE

How much texture you have in these soups is a matter of personal preference; the recipes are written according to how I like to eat them, but I'm just one person. In general, I think some soups should be thoroughly pureed, while others retain articulated ingredients.

But it's entirely up to you. If you like soups chunky, then don't puree them at all. If you want to be able to sip them from plastic cups at a picnic rather than serve them with a spoon, puree everything.

While I've given instructions to puree in a food processor fitted with the steel blade or in a blender, I must admit to being addicted to my immersion blender for this task. It resembles a long stick with the base of a blender, and you put it right into the pot of hot soup. While I don't advocate buying equipment for one job, if you really like pureed foods, it's worth the money.

Cheddar Cheese Soup

This soup is a first cousin to the classic English dish Welsh rarebit. It includes lots of cheddar cheese that's melted in beer, but in this case it also has vegetables.

Yield: 6–8 servings | **Active time:** 15 minutes | **Start to finish:** 30 minutes

3 tablespoons unsalted butter
1 medium onion, peeled and chopped
1 carrot, peeled and chopped
2 celery ribs, rinsed, trimmed, and chopped
3 tablespoons all-purpose flour
1 tablespoon paprika
1 (12-ounce) can lager beer
2 tablespoons chopped fresh parsley
1 tablespoon Worcestershire sauce
1 teaspoon dry mustard powder
1 bay leaf
3 cups half-and-half or whole milk
2 cups grated sharp cheddar cheese
Salt and freshly ground black pepper to taste

1. Heat butter in a 4-quart saucepan over medium heat. Add onion, carrot, and celery, and cook, stirring frequently, for 3 minutes, or until onion is translucent. Stir in flour and paprika, reduce the heat to low, and cook for 1 minute, stirring constantly.
2. Whisk in beer, and bring to a boil over high heat, stirring occasionally. Stir in parsley, Worcestershire sauce, mustard, and bay leaf. Reduce the heat to low, cover the pan, and simmer soup for 12–15 minutes, or until vegetables are tender. Add half-and-half, bring back to a boil, and simmer 2 minutes. Remove and discard bay leaf.
3. Add cheese to soup by ½-cup measures, stirring until cheese melts before adding additional cheese. Season to taste with salt and pepper, and serve immediately.

Note: The soup can be prepared up to 2 days in advance and refrigerated, tightly covered. Reheat it over low heat, covered, until hot, stirring occasionally. Do not allow it to boil.

Variations:

- Cook 1/4 pound bacon in a skillet over medium-high heat for 5–7 minutes, or until crisp. Remove bacon from the pan, drain well, and crumble. Substitute 3 tablespoons bacon grease for butter, and sprinkle crumbled bacon on each serving.
- Substitute chili powder for the paprika and substitute jalapeño Jack for the cheddar cheese. Omit the Worcestershire sauce and mustard.
- Substitute dry white wine for the beer.

Whenever you're adding cheese to a soup, stew, or sauce, always add it gradually. That way the cheese becomes incorporated into the mixture evenly and easily. If you add it all at once, it will need to be whisked briskly, and that will crush the vegetables.

Broccoli Cheddar Soup

This is one of my favorite soups; it's like broccoli in cheese sauce but in a soup form. It's a wonderful first course for a roast chicken dinner in the fall.

Yield: 6–8 servings | **Active time:** 15 minutes | **Start to finish:** 30 minutes

3 tablespoons unsalted butter
1 medium onion, peeled and chopped
2 tablespoons all-purpose flour
3 cups Chicken Stock (recipe on page 23) or purchased stock
1 (1-pound) package frozen chopped broccoli
2 tablespoons chopped fresh parsley
½ cup heavy cream
1½ cups grated sharp cheddar cheese
Salt and freshly ground black pepper to taste

1. Heat butter in a 4-quart saucepan over medium-high heat. Add onion, and cook, stirring frequently, for 3 minutes, or until onion is translucent. Stir in flour, reduce the heat to low, and cook for 1 minute, stirring constantly.
2. Whisk in stock, and bring to a boil over high heat, stirring occasionally. Stir in broccoli and parsley, and return to a boil. Reduce the heat to low, cover the pan, and simmer soup for 12–15 minutes, or until vegetables are tender. Add cream, and simmer 2 minutes.
3. Remove 2 cups of solids from the pan with a slotted spoon. Combine solids and cheese in a food processor fitted with the steel blade or in a blender. Be careful not to fill the beaker too full when blending hot ingredients. Puree until smooth, and stir puree back into soup. Season to taste with salt and pepper, and serve immediately.

Note: The soup can be prepared up to 2 days in advance and refrigerated, tightly covered. Reheat it over low heat, covered, until hot, stirring occasionally.

Variations:

- Substitute cauliflower or spinach for the broccoli.
- Substitute Swiss cheese for the cheddar.

Italian Egg and Cheese Soup *(Stracciatella)*

Stracciatella means "little rags" in Italian, and that's because the strands of egg in the soup look like shreds of cloth. Unlike the Chinese-American version of egg drop soup, which is thickened with cornstarch, this Italian version is thin, so the egg strands sink to the bottom of the bowl.

Yield: 6–8 servings | **Active time:** 10 minutes | **Start to finish:** 20 minutes

1 (10-ounce) package frozen chopped spinach, thawed
5 cups Chicken Stock (recipe on page 23) or purchased stock
2 tablespoons chopped fresh parsley
½ teaspoon Italian seasoning
½ cup freshly grated Parmesan cheese
3 large eggs, lightly beaten
Salt and freshly ground black pepper to taste

1. Place spinach in a colander, and press with the back of a spoon to extract as much liquid as possible.
2. Combine spinach, stock, parsley, and Italian seasoning in a 4-quart saucepan, and bring to a boil over medium-high heat, stirring occasionally. Reduce the heat to low, and simmer soup, covered, for 3 minutes. Add cheese, and simmer for an additional 2 minutes.
3. Slowly add eggs to simmering soup while stirring gently but constantly. Cook for 1 minute. Season to taste with salt and pepper, and serve immediately.

Note: The soup can be prepared up to 2 days in advance and refrigerated, tightly covered. Reheat it over low heat, covered, until hot, stirring occasionally.

Variation:

- Substitute 1 bunch fresh kale, rinsed, stemmed, and shredded, for the spinach.

French Split Pea Soup *(Potage Saint-Germain)*

While I think of basic split pea soup as a hearty winter dish, this version is light enough to serve in the spring and summer, too. The combination of split peas with a light cream, fresh peas, and other vegetables truly lightens both the color and flavor.

Yield: 6–8 servings | **Active time:** 20 minutes | **Start to finish:** 1½ hours

2 cups dried split peas
7 cups Chicken Stock (recipe on page 23) or purchased stock, divided
2 tablespoons unsalted butter
2 medium onions, peeled and chopped
1 carrot, peeled and chopped
2 celery ribs, rinsed, trimmed, and chopped
1 cup shredded lettuce, rinsed and dried
1 cup frozen peas, thawed
2 tablespoons chopped fresh parsley
1 teaspoon dried thyme
1 bay leaf
1 cup half-and-half or whole milk
Salt and freshly ground black pepper to taste

1. Place split peas in a colander, and rinse well under cold running water. Place split peas and 5 cups stock in a 4-quart saucepan, and bring to a boil over medium-high heat, stirring occasionally. Reduce the heat to low, and simmer split peas, covered, for 35–40 minutes, or until most of stock is absorbed.
2. While split peas simmer, heat butter in a skillet over medium-high heat. Add onion, carrot, and celery, and cook, stirring frequently, for 3 minutes, or until onion is translucent.
3. Add remaining 2 cups stock, vegetable mixture, lettuce, peas, parsley, thyme, and bay leaf to the split peas. Bring to a boil over medium-high heat, then reduce the heat to low, and simmer soup, covered, for 30–40 minutes, or until vegetables are tender and split peas have disintegrated.

4. Remove and discard bay leaf, and puree soup in a food processor fitted with the steel blade or in a blender. Be careful not to fill the beaker too full when blending hot ingredients. Return to the pan, and stir in half-and-half. Heat to a simmer, season to taste with salt and pepper, and serve immediately.

Note: The soup can be prepared up to 2 days in advance and refrigerated, tightly covered. Reheat it over low heat, covered, until hot, stirring occasionally.

> Along with lentils, split peas are the one form of dried legume that does not benefit from any presoaking. They cook very quickly, but you should make sure the heat is very low because they have a tendency to scorch.

Dilled Cream of Cucumber Soup

Aromatic dill and delicate cucumber are natural partners, and this is a soup that can be served either hot or cold. While I find cucumber seeds distracting, the soup's even quicker to make if you don't bother seeding the cucumbers.

Yield: 6–8 servings | **Active time:** 15 minutes | **Start to finish:** 35 minutes

4 tablespoons (½ stick) unsalted butter, divided
2 large or 3 small cucumbers, peeled, seeded, and sliced
¼ cup chopped fresh dill, divided
3 cups Chicken Stock (recipe on page 23) or purchased stock
3 tablespoons all-purpose flour
1 cup half-and-half
Salt and freshly ground black pepper to taste
Fresh dill sprigs for garnish (optional)

1. Melt 2 tablespoons butter in a 4-quart saucepan over medium heat. Add cucumber and ½ of dill. Cook, stirring occasionally, for 5 minutes.
2. Add stock, and bring to a boil over high heat. Reduce the heat to low, and simmer soup, partially covered, for 15–20 minutes, or until cucumbers are soft.
3. While soup simmers, melt remaining 2 tablespoons butter in a small saucepan over low heat. Add flour, and cook for 2 minutes, stirring constantly. Whisk in half-and-half, raise the heat to medium, and cook until mixture comes to a simmer, stirring frequently. Add mixture to soup, and simmer 2 minutes.
4. Puree soup in a food processor fitted with the steel blade or in a blender. Be careful not to fill the beaker too full when blending hot ingredients. Stir in remaining dill, and season to taste with salt and pepper. To serve, ladle soup into bowls and top with dill sprigs, if using.

Note: The soup can be made up to 2 days in advance and refrigerated, tightly covered. Reheat it over low heat, covered, until hot, stirring occasionally.

Variation:

- Substitute chopped fresh basil or oregano for the dill.

Coconut Pumpkin Soup

Creamy sweet coconut milk and aromatic and assertive Asian spices elevate all-American pumpkin to a new level of sophistication in this quick and easy soup.

Yield: 6–8 servings | **Active time:** 15 minutes | **Start to finish:** 35 minutes

3 tablespoons unsalted butter
1 medium onion, peeled and chopped
2 garlic cloves, peeled and minced
2 tablespoons grated fresh ginger
3 cups canned solid-pack pumpkin
2 cups Chicken Stock (recipe on page 23) or purchased stock
2 tablespoons soy sauce
1 tablespoon firmly packed dark brown sugar
1 teaspoon Chinese chile paste with garlic*
½ teaspoon Chinese five-spice powder*
1 (14-ounce) can light coconut milk
Salt and freshly ground black pepper to taste
½–¾ cup shredded coconut, toasted in a 350°F oven for 5–7 minutes, or until lightly browned (optional)

1. Heat butter in a 4-quart saucepan over medium heat. Add onion, garlic, and ginger, and cook, stirring frequently, for 3 minutes, or until onion is translucent.
2. Add pumpkin, stock, soy sauce, brown sugar, chile paste, and five-spice powder, and bring to a boil, stirring frequently. Reduce the heat to low, and cook soup, covered, for 15 minutes.
3. Stir in coconut milk, and simmer for 2 minutes. Season to taste with salt and pepper, and serve immediately, sprinkling each serving with toasted coconut, if using.

Note: The soup can be prepared up to 2 days in advance and refrigerated, tightly covered. Reheat it over low heat, covered, until hot, stirring occasionally.

Variation:

- Substitute cooked acorn or butternut squash for the pumpkin.

*Available in the Asian aisle of most supermarkets and in specialty markets.

Asian-Spiced Acorn Squash Soup

Many years ago I began experimenting with fusion cuisine, which is a joining of Asian and Western forms and ingredients. This soup is emblematic of that style, with hoisin sauce and five-spice powder enlivening a Western soup.

Yield: 6–8 servings | **Active time:** 15 minutes | **Start to finish:** 1¾ hours

- 3 pounds (2 medium) acorn squash
- 2 cups Chicken Stock (recipe on page 23) or purchased stock
- 2 scallions, white parts and 4 inches of green tops, rinsed, trimmed, and chopped
- 3 tablespoons hoisin sauce*
- 2 tablespoons rum
- ¼ teaspoon Chinese five-spice powder*
- 1 cup half-and-half or whole milk
- Salt and freshly ground black pepper to taste

1. Preheat the oven to 400°F, and line a baking pan with aluminum foil.
2. Prick squash with a sharp meat fork. Bake squash for 1 hour, or until the flesh is tender when probed with a sharp meat fork, turning occasionally during baking. Cut squash in half, discard seeds, and scrape flesh from shell. Cut flesh into 2-inch chunks.
3. Combine squash, stock, scallions, hoisin sauce, rum, and five-spice powder in a 4-quart saucepan. Bring to a boil over medium heat and simmer, partially covered, for 20 minutes.
4. Puree soup in a food processor fitted with the steel blade or in a blender. Be careful not to fill the beaker too full when blending hot ingredients. Return soup to the pan, and add half-and-half. Bring to a boil over medium heat, stirring frequently, and simmer over low heat for 5 minutes. Season to taste with salt and pepper, and serve immediately.

Note: The soup can be prepared up to 2 days in advance and refrigerated, tightly covered. Reheat it over low heat, covered, until hot, stirring occasionally.

*Available in the Asian aisle of most supermarkets and in specialty markets.

Variation:

- Substitute molasses, bourbon, and cinnamon for the hoisin sauce, rum, and Chinese five-spice powder for an American flavor.

When choosing acorn squash, pick one heavy for its size with no blemishes on the skin. Butternut squash can be substituted in any recipe calling for acorn squash.

Curried Carrot Soup

The natural sweetness of carrots, rich in beta-carotene to boost your immune system, is actually accentuated when contrasted with a bit of curry in this quick and easy soup.

Yield: 6–8 servings | **Active time:** 15 minutes | **Start to finish:** 45 minutes

4 tablespoons (½ stick) unsalted butter, divided
6 large carrots, peeled and sliced
1 medium onion, peeled and sliced
½ large apple, peeled and sliced
1½–2 tablespoons curry powder
¼ teaspoon ground cinnamon
4 cups Chicken Stock (recipe on page 23) or purchased stock
3 tablespoons all-purpose flour
2 cups half-and-half or whole milk
Salt and freshly ground black pepper to taste

1. Melt 2 tablespoons butter in a 4-quart saucepan over medium heat. Add carrots, onion, and apple, and cook, stirring frequently, for 10 minutes. Stir in curry powder and cinnamon, reduce the heat to low, and cook for 1 minute, stirring constantly.
2. Raise the heat to medium, and slowly stir in stock. Bring to a boil and simmer soup over low heat, uncovered, for 20 minutes.
3. While soup simmers, melt remaining 2 tablespoons butter in a small saucepan over low heat. Add flour, and cook for 2 minutes, stirring constantly. Whisk in half-and-half, raise the heat to medium, and cook until mixture comes to a simmer, stirring frequently. Add mixture to soup, and simmer 2 minutes, or until carrots are very tender.
4. Puree soup in a food processor fitted with the steel blade or in a blender. Be careful not to fill the beaker too full when blending hot ingredients. Season to taste with salt and pepper, and serve immediately.

Note: The soup can be made up to 2 days in advance and refrigerated, tightly covered. Serve it cold, or reheat it over low heat, covered, until hot, stirring occasionally.

Variation:

- Substitute parsnips for the carrots and the soup will be even sweeter.

Cream of Celery Soup with Tarragon

Tarragon is an elegant herb with a slight anise, or licorice, flavor. This soup is subtly seasoned, and the rice used for thickening creates a luscious texture.

Yield: 6–8 servings | **Active time:** 10 minutes | **Start to finish:** 55 minutes

5 cups (about 2/3 bunch) rinsed, trimmed, and sliced celery
3 1/2 cups Chicken Stock (recipe on page 23) or purchased stock
1/2 cup white rice
2 teaspoons dried tarragon
1 1/2 cups half-and-half or whole milk
Salt and freshly ground black pepper to taste

1. Combine celery, stock, rice, and tarragon in a 4-quart saucepan. Bring to a boil over high heat, stirring occasionally. Reduce the heat to low, and simmer soup, partially covered, for 30 minutes.
2. Puree soup in a food processor fitted with the steel blade or in a blender. Be careful not to fill the beaker too full when blending hot ingredients. Return soup to the pan, stir in half-and-half, and simmer 2 minutes. Season to taste with salt and pepper, and serve immediately.

Note: The soup can be prepared up to 2 days in advance and refrigerated, tightly covered. Reheat it over low heat, covered, until hot, stirring occasionally.

Variations:

- Substitute sliced raw fennel for the celery to accentuate the flavor of the tarragon.
- Substitute 1/4 cup chopped fresh dill for the tarragon.

Dilled Vegetable Chowder

The aromatic dill in this soup gives it a light feel in your mouth, while the potatoes and other vegetables create a hearty context.

Yield: 6–8 servings | **Active time:** 15 minutes | **Start to finish:** 40 minutes

3 tablespoons unsalted butter
1 medium onion, peeled and diced
1 large carrot, peeled and diced
2 celery ribs, rinsed, trimmed, and diced
2 large baking potatoes, peeled and cut into ¾-inch dice
4 cups Chicken Stock (recipe on page 23) or purchased stock
1 tablespoon chopped fresh parsley
1 cup half-and-half or whole milk
¾ cup frozen peas, thawed
¼ cup chopped fresh dill
Salt and freshly ground black pepper to taste

1. Heat butter in a 4-quart saucepan over medium-high heat. Add onion, carrot, and celery, and cook, stirring frequently, for 3 minutes, or until onion is translucent.
2. Add potatoes, stock, and parsley, and bring to a boil over high heat, stirring occasionally. Reduce the heat to low, and cook, covered, for 15–20 minutes, or until vegetables are tender.
3. Remove ⅓ of solids from the pan with a slotted spoon, and puree in a food processor fitted with the steel blade or in a blender. Be careful not to fill the beaker too full when blending hot ingredients. Return puree to the pan, and add half-and-half, peas, and dill.
4. Bring back to a boil, and simmer for 3 minutes. Season to taste with salt and pepper, and serve immediately.

Note: The soup can be prepared up to 2 days in advance and refrigerated, tightly covered. Reheat it over low heat, covered, until hot, stirring occasionally.

Variation:

- Add 1 cup grated Swiss cheese or sharp cheddar cheese along with the half-and-half.

Creamy Onion and Potato Soup

I invented this soup because it includes two of my all-time favorite foods—sweet caramelized onions and creamy potatoes. It's fantastic before a chunky beef stew or a pot roast.

Yield: 6–8 servings | **Active time:** 20 minutes | **Start to finish:** 1 hour

4 tablespoons (1/2 stick) unsalted butter
2 tablespoons olive oil
3 large sweet onions, such as Bermuda or Vidalia, peeled and diced
1 teaspoon granulated sugar
Salt and freshly ground black pepper to taste
4 cups Chicken Stock (recipe on page 23) or purchased stock
1 tablespoon chopped fresh parsley
1/2 teaspoon dried thyme
1 1/2 pounds russet potatoes, peeled and diced
1 cup half-and-half or whole milk

1. Melt butter and oil in a large skillet over medium heat. Add onions, sugar, salt, and pepper, and toss to coat onions. Cover the skillet, and cook for 10 minutes, stirring occasionally. Uncover the skillet, and cook over medium-high heat for 20–30 minutes, or until onions are browned. Remove 1/2 cup onions, and set aside. Transfer remaining onions to a 4-quart saucepan.
2. Add stock, parsley, thyme, and potatoes to the pan, and bring to a boil over high heat, stirring occasionally. Reduce the heat to low, and simmer soup, covered, for 15–20 minutes, or until potatoes are very tender, stirring occasionally.
3. Puree soup in a food processor fitted with the steel blade or in a blender. Be careful not to fill the beaker too full when blending hot ingredients. Stir in half-and-half, and season to taste with salt and pepper. Serve immediately, sprinkling each serving with reserved onions.

Note: The soup can be prepared up to 2 days in advance and refrigerated, tightly covered. Reheat it over low heat, covered, until hot, stirring occasionally.

Variation:

- Add 1 head roasted garlic to the soup; see page 58 for the method of roasting the garlic.

Potato Soup with Gorgonzola and Pancetta

This is a creamy and sophisticated soup that is wonderful to serve as a first course for any nouvelle, or even classic, Italian meal. The potato soup is laced with flavorful Gorgonzola cheese and then topped by bits of crunchy pancetta.

Yield: 6–8 servings | **Active time:** 20 minutes | **Start to finish:** 45 minutes

- 1/4 pound pancetta, finely chopped
- 1 large onion, peeled and chopped
- 1 carrot, peeled and chopped
- 1 celery rib, rinsed, trimmed, and chopped
- 1/2 cup dry white wine
- 3 1/2 cups Chicken Stock (recipe on page 23) or purchased stock
- 2 tablespoons chopped fresh parsley
- 1/2 teaspoon Italian seasoning
- 1 bay leaf
- 3/4 pound russet potatoes, peeled and chopped
- 3/4 cup crumbled Gorgonzola cheese
- 3/4 cup half-and-half or whole milk
- Salt and freshly ground black pepper to taste

1. Place pancetta in a 4-quart saucepan, and cook over medium-high heat for 4–6 minutes, or until pancetta is crisp. Remove pancetta from the pan with a slotted spoon, and set aside. Discard all but 2 tablespoons of fat from the pan.
2. Add onion, carrot, and celery to the pan, and cook, stirring frequently, for 3 minutes, or until onion is translucent. Add wine, and cook for 2 minutes. Add stock, parsley, Italian seasoning, bay leaf, and potato. Bring to a boil over high heat, stirring occasionally.
3. Reduce the heat to low, cover the pan, and cook for 15–20 minutes, or until vegetables are very soft. Remove and discard bay leaf.
4. Remove 1 cup of solids from the pan with a slotted spoon. Combine solids and cheese in a food processor fitted with the steel blade or in a blender. Be careful not to fill the beaker too full when blending hot ingredients. Puree until smooth, and stir puree back into soup. Add half-and-half to the pan, and bring back just to a simmer; do not let it boil. Season to taste with salt and pepper, and serve immediately, sprinkling each serving with pancetta.

Note: The soup can be prepared up to 2 days in advance and refrigerated, tightly covered. Reheat it over low heat, covered, until hot, stirring occasionally. Refrigerate pancetta, and reheat in a microwave oven before serving.

Variations:

- Substitute bacon for the pancetta.
- Substitute blue cheese or Stilton cheese for the Gorgonzola.

> There's a reason why bay leaves should always be discarded. Although they add a pungent and woodsy flavor and aroma to dishes, they can be quite a bitter mouthful if you accidentally eat one. That's also why bay leaves are always added whole. If they were broken into pieces, it would be a real scavenger hunt to retrieve them.

Garlic Soup

No vampires lurking after you've eaten this soup; it contains both nutty roasted garlic *and* sweet poached garlic in a broth flavored with herbs and heady Parmesan cheese.

Yield: 6–8 servings | **Active time:** 20 minutes | **Start to finish:** 1¾ hours

2 heads garlic
3 tablespoons unsalted butter
1 large onion, peeled and diced
5 cups Chicken Stock (recipe on page 23) or purchased stock
3 tablespoons tomato paste
12 garlic cloves, peeled
1½ teaspoons herbes de Provence
⅔ cup freshly grated Parmesan cheese
Salt and freshly ground black pepper to taste

1. Preheat the oven to 350°F. Cut ¼ inch off tops of garlic heads. Discard tops. Wrap heads tightly in foil, and place heads on a baking sheet. Roast garlic for 1 hour, or until tender. When cool enough to handle, break heads apart into cloves and press flesh out of cloves. Set aside.
2. While garlic roasts, melt butter in a 4-quart saucepan over medium heat. Add onion, and cook, stirring frequently, for 5 minutes, or until onion softens.
3. Add stock, tomato paste, garlic cloves, and herbes de Provence to the pan, and stir well to dissolve tomato paste. Bring to a boil over high heat, stirring occasionally. Reduce the heat to low, cover the pan, and cook for 12–15 minutes, or until onion is tender.
4. Strain solids from soup, and combine with roasted garlic and cheese in a food processor fitted with the steel blade or in a blender. Be careful not to fill the beaker too full when blending hot ingredients. Puree until smooth, and stir mixture back into broth. Season to taste with salt and pepper, and serve immediately.

Note: The soup can be prepared up to 2 days in advance and refrigerated, tightly covered. Reheat it over low heat, covered, until hot, stirring occasionally.

Variation:

- Transform this into an entree soup by adding 1–2 poached eggs to each serving.

> The way you treat garlic determines the intensity of its flavor. Pushing the cloves through a garlic press is the way to extract the most punch; mincing the cloves once they're peeled produces a milder flavor. Roasting or poaching garlic, as in this soup, produces an almost sweet result.

Roasted Garlic Vichyssoise

Vichyssoise, actually an American invention despite the French name, is the grandma of all cold summer soups. Chef Louis Diat created it during his tenure at the Ritz-Carlton Hotel in New York. Diat named the soup after Vichy, the resort town near his boyhood home in France. The combination of delicate leeks and onions with creamy potatoes can't be beaten, except by adding sweet roasted garlic.

Yield: 6–8 servings | **Active time:** 15 minutes | **Start to finish:** 2¾ hours, including 2 hours for chilling

- 1–2 heads fresh garlic
- 3 tablespoons unsalted butter
- 4 leeks, white parts and 2 inches of light green tops, rinsed well, trimmed, and chopped
- 1 small onion, peeled and chopped
- 1½ pounds boiling potatoes, peeled and thinly sliced
- 6 cups Chicken Stock (recipe on page 23) or purchased stock
- ¾ cup heavy cream
- Salt and freshly ground black pepper to taste
- ¼ cup chopped chives for garnish

1. Preheat the oven to 350°F. Cut ¼ inch off top of garlic. Discard top. Wrap head tightly in foil, and place head on a baking sheet. Roast garlic for 1 hour, or until tender. When cool enough to handle, break head apart into cloves and press flesh out of cloves. Set aside.
2. While garlic roasts, melt butter in a 4-quart saucepan over medium heat. Add leeks and onion, and cook, stirring frequently, for 5 minutes, or until onion is translucent. Add potatoes and stock, and bring to a boil over high heat. Reduce the heat to low, and simmer soup, partially covered, for 25 minutes, or until potatoes are tender.
3. Add garlic to soup, and puree soup in a food processor fitted with the steel blade or in a blender. Be careful not to fill the beaker too full when blending hot ingredients. Stir in cream, and season to taste with salt and pepper. Refrigerate until cold, at least 2 hours. To serve, ladle soup into bowls, sprinkling each serving with chopped chives.

Note: The soup can be made up to 2 days in advance and refrigerated, tightly covered. Stir it well before serving.

Variations:

- Omit the garlic for a classic vichyssoise.
- Omit the cream, and increase the chicken stock by 3/4 cup. Instead of pureeing the soup, mash some of it with a potato masher and serve it hot.
- Add 2 cups frozen peas, thawed.

> You can always substitute finely chopped green scallion tops for chives in any recipe. It's rare that you ever use a whole scallion, so they frequently go to waste.

Gazpacho

It wouldn't be summer without a vat of this Spanish soup in my refrigerator. My version is spicy and contains some mellow vinegar to balance the innate sweetness of the tomatoes. I keep the soup rather chunky and rustic, but if you prefer a smoother texture, puree more of the vegetables. Without the oil, this also makes the best Bloody Mary mix you'll ever drink.

Yield: 6–8 servings | **Active time:** 15 minutes | **Start to finish:** 2¼ hours, including 2 hours for chilling

½–1 sweet onion, such as Bermuda or Vidalia, peeled and diced
1 small cucumber, peeled, seeded, and cut into 1-inch sections
1 green bell pepper, seeds and ribs removed, diced
3 medium to large ripe tomatoes, seeded and diced, divided
2 garlic cloves, peeled
1 cup tomato juice
3 tablespoons olive oil
1 jalapeño or serrano chile, seeds and ribs removed, diced
3 tablespoons balsamic vinegar
¼ cup chopped fresh cilantro
Salt and freshly ground black pepper to taste

1. Finely chop onion, cucumber, green bell pepper, and 1 tomato in a food processor. Scrape the mixture into a large bowl.
2. Puree remaining tomatoes, garlic, tomato juice, olive oil, chile, and vinegar in a food processor fitted with the steel blade or in a blender. Stir puree into vegetables, add cilantro, and season to taste with salt and pepper. Refrigerate until cold, at least 2 hours.

Note: The soup can be prepared up to 2 days in advance and refrigerated, tightly covered. Stir it well before serving.

Variation:

- Substitute orange tomatoes for the red tomatoes, orange bell pepper for the green bell pepper, and carrot juice for the tomato juice. Increase the balsamic vinegar to ¼ cup.

Chilled Pea Soup with Tarragon

Serving a cold soup made from fresh peas is an English tradition, but I like the anise-scented tarragon better than the traditional mint.

Yield: 6–8 servings | **Active time:** 15 minutes | **Start to finish:** 2½ hours, including 2 hours for chilling

2 tablespoons unsalted butter
1 medium onion, peeled and chopped
4 cups Chicken Stock (recipe on page 23) or purchased stock
¾ pound boiling potatoes, peeled and cut into 1-inch dice
2 (10-ounce) packages frozen peas, thawed
2 tablespoons chopped fresh parsley
1 tablespoon dried tarragon
1 cup half-and-half
Salt and freshly ground black pepper to taste
½–¾ cup sour cream or crème fraîche

1. Heat butter in a 4-quart saucepan over medium-high heat. Add onion, and cook, stirring frequently, for 3 minutes, or until onion is translucent.
2. Add stock, potatoes, peas, parsley, and tarragon to the pan, and bring to a boil over high heat, stirring occasionally. Reduce the heat to low, and simmer soup, covered, for 15–20 minutes, or until potatoes are very tender.
3. Puree soup in a food processor fitted with the steel blade or in a blender. Be careful not to fill the beaker too full when blending hot ingredients. Stir in half-and-half, and season to taste with salt and pepper.
4. Refrigerate until cold, at least 2 hours. Adjust seasoning, if necessary. To serve, ladle soup into bowls, topping each serving with sour cream.

Note: The soup can be prepared up to 2 days in advance and refrigerated, tightly covered. Reheat it over low heat, covered, until hot, stirring occasionally.

Variation:

- Use ½ cup firmly packed fresh mint leaves instead of the tarragon.

Chilled Cream of Zucchini Soup with Basil

This thick soup is a natural for summer, when both zucchini and fresh basil are plentiful in the markets, if not in your garden or on your terrace. The texture comes from the large amount of zucchini used in the puree.

Yield: 6–8 servings | **Active time:** 15 minutes | **Start to finish:** 2¾ hours, including 2 hours for chilling

3 tablespoons unsalted butter
1 small onion, peeled and chopped
2 pounds small zucchini, rinsed, trimmed, and thinly sliced
3 cups Chicken Stock (recipe on page 23) or purchased stock
½ cup firmly packed fresh basil leaves
1 cup half-and-half
½ cup sour cream or plain nonfat yogurt
Salt and freshly ground black pepper to taste
6 fresh basil sprigs for garnish (optional)

1. Melt butter in a 4-quart saucepan over medium-high heat. Add onion and cook, stirring frequently, for 3 minutes, or until onion is translucent.
2. Add zucchini and stock, and bring to a boil over high heat. Reduce the heat to low, and simmer soup, partially covered, for 20 minutes, or until zucchini is soft.
3. Stir in basil, and puree soup in a food processor fitted with the steel blade or in a blender. Be careful not to fill the beaker too full when blending hot ingredients. Stir in half-and-half and sour cream, and season to taste with salt and pepper. Refrigerate until cold, at least 2 hours. To serve, ladle soup into bowls and top with basil sprigs, if using.

Note: The soup can be made up to 2 days in advance and refrigerated, tightly covered. Stir it well before serving.

Variation:

- For a more intensely flavored soup, add 2 garlic cloves, peeled and minced. Sauté the garlic with the onions.

Chapter 4:

Versatile Vegetarian: Meatless Soups and Stews

Even if you eat meat on a regular basis, you—like me—may count yourself among the ranks of the "occasional vegetarian." Especially if I've been indulging in a lot of rich food, it seems that my stomach reacts well to a few nights in the vegetable patch. Those are the recipes you'll find in this chapter.

But you'll be hard pressed to term any of these luscious dishes "bunny food." They are thick in texture and richly flavored. They are made with a cornucopia of vividly colored fresh vegetables, plus some equally nutritious frozen vegetables when appropriate.

Unlike canned vegetables, from which much of the nutrition is robbed by the heating process, I have no objection to various frozen vegetables, especially ones such as peas, green beans, and spinach, which are far less expensive in their frozen form, ounce for ounce. So don't feel guilty if you use frozen vegetables. It's equivalent to using dried herbs and spices. Fresh might be better, but it's hardly a necessity.

Also, for foods like corn kernels, the flavor is far superior when frozen fresh from the field instead of eating tasteless corn out of season.

THOSE LOVELY LEGUMES

Beans are justly praised for their nutritional value as well as their availability and economy, and dried beans play a role in almost all the world's cuisines. Beans are a good source of fiber and protein, and they are low in fat and contain no cholesterol. They are also a good source of B vitamins, especially B_6.

Before using dried beans, rinse them in a colander or sieve under cold running water, and pick through them to discard any broken beans or pebbles that might have found their way into the bag. Then there's a secondary step once the beans have been covered with water: Discard any that float to the top.

Dried beans should be cooked until they are no longer crunchy but still have texture. If beans are going to be cooked and then cooked further in a dish, such as in a chili, then stop the initial cooking when they are still slightly crunchy. The other caveat of bean cookery is to make sure beans are cooked to the proper consistency before adding any acidic ingredient—such as tomatoes, vinegar, or lemon—because acid makes it take longer for beans to soften. Cooking times in these recipes vary quite a lot because of when the acid is added.

Cooking beans is common sense; the larger the bean, the longer it will take to soften. But it's not necessary to presoak larger beans for a longer period of time than smaller beans. There's only so much softening that goes on at no or low heat.

Once you've soaked the beans, always discard the soaking liquid, and place the beans in a saucepan. If using a recipe, the amount of liquid to add is included.

There are other reasons why beans can take longer to cook. Beans that are a few years old will take longer. Also, the minerals in your tap water can retard the softening and require a longer cooking time.

BEAN SUBSTITUTION CHART

Bean recipes are very tolerant to substitutions, but color, texture, and flavor should be considered. Use this chart for guidance.

Bean	What to Substitute
Black (also called turtle)	Kidney
Black-eyed peas	Kidney
Cannellini	Navy
Cranberry (also called borlotti)	Kidney
Fava (broad beans)	Large lima
Flageolet	Navy
Kidney (pink and red, pinto)	Navy
Lentils (red, brown, green)	Split peas
Split peas	Lentils

COMPLETING THE PROTEIN

While Americans have eaten too much animal protein in recent decades, protein itself is an essential part of a healthy diet. A complete protein, such as that found in meats, eggs, dairy, poultry, and fish, is one that contains all essential amino acids. Foods such as beans and rice are incomplete proteins, but if eaten together they become a complete protein.

While it used to be assumed that the two complementary proteins had to be eaten at the same meal, nutritional authorities now say that eating them within the same day will accomplish the creation of a complete protein. If following a vegetarian diet, beans, nuts, and soy products are all excellent sources of proteins; however, nuts are also high in calories.

SPEEDING UP THE PROCESS

Here are the benefits of dry beans: They're less expensive, they don't have the high sodium content of canned beans, you can monitor their texture, and you can flavor them as you wish. Here is the benefit of canned beans: They're ready to use because they're already cooked.

There is a basic arithmetic to dry and cooked beans: ⅔ cup of dry beans, when cooked, is equal to the contents of 1 (15-ounce) can cooked beans. So calculate accordingly. But do add the canned beans at the end of the cooking time, because they're already fully cooked.

Garden Vegetable Soup

This soup is like a whole vegetable garden put into your bowl. The vegetables are cooked gently, so they retain their individual textures as well as flavors. Serve this with one of the flavored muffin recipes you'll find in Chapter 8.

Yield: 4–6 servings | **Active time:** 15 minutes | **Start to finish:** 45 minutes

- 7 cups Vegetable Stock (recipe on page 25) or purchased stock
- 3 sprigs fresh parsley
- 2 garlic cloves, peeled and halved
- 1 tablespoon herbes de Provence
- 2 tablespoons olive oil
- 1 medium onion, peeled and diced
- 2 carrots, peeled and sliced
- 1 red bell pepper, seeds and ribs removed, diced
- 2 cups cauliflower florets, cut into 3/4-inch pieces
- 2 medium zucchini, rinsed, trimmed, and cut into 3/4-inch cubes
- Salt and freshly ground black pepper to taste

1. Combine stock, parsley, garlic, and herbes de Provence in a 4-quart saucepan, and bring to a boil over high heat, stirring occasionally. Reduce the heat to low, and simmer stock, uncovered, for 10 minutes. Strain stock through a sieve lined with a paper coffee filter or a paper towel. Return stock to the pan.
2. While stock simmers, heat oil in a small skillet over medium-high heat. Add onion, and cook, stirring frequently, for 3 minutes, or until onion is translucent. Set aside.
3. Add onion, carrots, bell pepper, and cauliflower to stock, and bring to a boil over high heat, stirring occasionally. Reduce the heat to low, and simmer soup, uncovered, for 12 minutes. Add zucchini, and simmer for an additional 8–10 minutes, or until vegetables are tender. Season to taste with salt and pepper, and serve immediately.

Note: The soup can be prepared up to 2 days in advance and refrigerated, tightly covered. Reheat it over low heat, covered, until hot, stirring occasionally.

Variation:

- Substitute broccoli for the cauliflower and yellow squash for the zucchini.

Zucchini is Italian in origin, and its native name was retained when it was integrated into American cooking. Choose small zucchini because they tend to have a sweeter flavor and the seeds are tender and less pronounced.

Southwestern Vegetable Soup

The clear broth in this bountiful soup is moderately spicy and loaded with flavor from the combination of aromatic herbs. Serve it with some cornbread, and the meal is complete.

Yield: 4–6 servings | **Active time:** 20 minutes | **Start to finish:** 40 minutes

3 tablespoons olive oil
1 large onion, peeled and diced
1 small poblano chile, seeds and ribs removed, chopped
2 garlic cloves, peeled and minced
1 jalapeño or serrano chile, seeds and ribs removed, finely chopped
2 teaspoons ground cumin
1 teaspoon dried oregano
5 cups Vegetable Stock (recipe on page 25) or purchased stock
¾ pound redskin potatoes, scrubbed and cut into 1-inch cubes
1 (15-ounce) can red kidney beans, drained and rinsed
1 (10-ounce) package frozen mixed vegetables, thawed
¼ cup chopped fresh cilantro
Salt and freshly ground black pepper to taste
Lime wedges

1. Heat oil in a 4-quart saucepan over medium-high heat. Add onion, poblano chile, garlic, and jalapeño chile. Cook, stirring frequently, for 3 minutes, or until onion is translucent. Add cumin and oregano, and cook for 1 minute, stirring constantly.
2. Stir in stock, and add potatoes. Bring to a boil over high heat, then reduce the heat to low, cover the pan, and cook for 12–15 minutes, or until potatoes are tender.
3. Coarsely mash potatoes with a potato masher. Stir in beans, mixed vegetables, and cilantro. Bring back to a boil and simmer, covered, for 3 minutes. Season to taste with salt and pepper, and serve immediately, garnishing each serving with lime wedges.

Note: The soup can be prepared up to 2 days in advance and refrigerated, tightly covered. Reheat it over low heat, covered, until hot, stirring occasionally.

Variation:

- Substitute sweet potatoes for the redskin potatoes, and omit the hot chile (jalapeño or serrano) for a milder soup.

It's common to see jalapeño and serrano chiles given as recipe options in the same quantity, although serrano peppers are much smaller. They are also much hotter, so the larger jalapeño and the smaller serrano produce the same amount of heat.

Basque Bean and Cabbage Soup (Garbure)

This traditional soup from the Basque region of Spain is usually made with ham hocks or sausage, but the smoked paprika adds the same smoky nuances—plus great color—to this vegetarian version.

Yield: 4–6 servings | **Active time:** 20 minutes | **Start to finish:** 3 hours, including 1 hour to soak beans

1½ cups dried white navy beans
2 tablespoons olive oil
1 medium onion, peeled and chopped
3 garlic cloves, peeled and minced
1 carrot, peeled and chopped
1 celery rib, rinsed, trimmed, and chopped
2 tablespoons smoked Spanish paprika
8 cups Vegetable Stock (recipe on page 25) or purchased stock
¼ cup chopped fresh parsley
1 teaspoon dried thyme
1 bay leaf
1 pound redskin potatoes, scrubbed and cut into 1-inch cubes
6 cups firmly packed shredded green cabbage
Salt and freshly ground black pepper to taste

1. Rinse beans in a colander and place them in a mixing bowl covered with cold water. Allow beans to soak overnight. Or place beans in a saucepan and bring to a boil over high heat. Boil 1 minute. Turn off the heat, cover the pan, and soak beans for 1 hour. With either soaking method, drain beans, discard soaking water, and begin cooking as soon as possible.
2. Heat oil in a 4-quart saucepan over medium-high heat. Add onion, garlic, carrot, and celery. Cook, stirring frequently, for 3 minutes, or until onion is translucent. Add paprika and cook for 1 minute, stirring constantly.
3. Add beans, stock, parsley, thyme, and bay leaf. Bring to a boil over high heat, then reduce the heat to low, and simmer soup, partially covered, for 45–50 minutes, or until beans are almost tender.

4. Add potatoes and cabbage, and cook for an additional 20–25 minutes, or until vegetables are very tender. Remove and discard bay leaf, season to taste with salt and pepper, and serve immediately.

Note: The soup can be prepared up to 2 days in advance and refrigerated, tightly covered. Reheat it over low heat, covered, until hot, stirring occasionally.

Variation:

- Omit the potatoes, and cook ½ pound macaroni or other small pasta in boiling salted water until al dente. Add them to the soup at the end of the cooking time.

Heat and light are the two worst enemies of dried herbs and spices, so a pretty display rack over the stove is about the worst place to store them. Keep them in a cool, dark place to preserve their potency. The best test for freshness and potency is to smell the contents. If you don't smell a strong aroma, you need a new bottle.

Vegetarian Minestrone

Every Italian soup filled with vegetables falls under the moniker of "minestrone," and this hearty version is part of that tradition. A tossed salad and a loaf of crusty bread complete your meal.

Yield: 4–6 servings | **Active time:** 20 minutes | **Start to finish:** 1 hour

- ¼ cup olive oil
- 1 medium onion, peeled and diced
- 1 large carrot, peeled and sliced
- 1 celery rib, rinsed, trimmed, and sliced
- 3 garlic cloves, peeled and minced
- 2 cups shredded green cabbage
- 5 cups Vegetable Stock (recipe on page 25) or purchased stock
- 1 (28-ounce) can diced tomatoes, undrained
- ¼ cup chopped fresh parsley
- 1 tablespoon Italian seasoning
- 2 zucchini, rinsed, trimmed, and diced
- ¼ pound green beans, trimmed and cut into ¾-inch pieces
- ¼ pound small shells or other small pasta
- Salt and freshly ground black pepper to taste
- ½ cup freshly grated Parmesan cheese

1. Heat olive oil in a 4-quart saucepan over medium-high heat. Add onion, carrot, celery, and garlic. Cook, stirring frequently, for 3 minutes, or until onion is translucent. Add cabbage, and cook for 1 minute.
2. Add stock, tomatoes, parsley, and Italian seasoning, and bring to a boil over medium-high heat, stirring occasionally. Reduce the heat to low, and simmer soup, partially covered, for 30 minutes. Add zucchini and green beans, and simmer for an additional 15 minutes.
3. While soup simmers, bring a large pot of salted water to a boil over high heat. Cook pasta according to package directions until al dente. Drain, and set aside.
4. Add pasta to soup, and season to taste with salt and pepper. Serve hot, passing Parmesan cheese separately.

Note: The soup can be prepared up to 2 days in advance and refrigerated, tightly covered. Reheat it over low heat, covered, until hot, stirring occasionally. If cooking it in advance, add the pasta when reheating it.

Variation:

- Substitute 1 (15-ounce) can garbanzo beans, drained and rinsed, for the zucchini.

I know I promised you one-pot cooking, but it really makes a difference to cook pasta by itself rather than cooking it in a soup. The starch from the pasta gives the soup broth an unappealing floury flavor.

Italian Bean and Pasta Soup

I adore this soup, and it's quintessential comfort food on a cold winter night. Serve a tossed salad with a garlicky vinaigrette dressing and you're set for dinner.

Yield: 6–8 servings | **Active time:** 20 minutes | **Start to finish:** 3½ hours, including 1 hour to soak beans

1 pound dried borlotti (cranberry) beans
½ cup olive oil, divided
2 large onions, peeled and chopped
1 teaspoon granulated sugar
Salt and freshly ground black pepper to taste
2 carrots, peeled and chopped
2 celery ribs, rinsed, trimmed, and chopped
6 garlic cloves
8 cups Vegetable Stock (recipe on page 25) or purchased stock
¼ cup chopped fresh parsley
1 tablespoon dried rosemary, crumbled
1 teaspoon Italian seasoning
1 bay leaf
1 (3-inch) piece Parmesan rind (optional)
½ pound small shells or other small pasta
½–¾ cup freshly grated Parmesan cheese

1. Rinse beans in a colander and place them in a mixing bowl covered with cold water. Allow beans to soak overnight. Or place beans in a saucepan and bring to a boil over high heat. Boil 1 minute. Turn off the heat, cover the pan, and soak beans for 1 hour. With either soaking method, drain beans, discard soaking water, and begin cooking as soon as possible.
2. Heat ¼ cup olive oil in a 4-quart saucepan over medium heat. Add onions, sugar, salt, and pepper, and toss to coat onions. Cover the pan, and cook for 10 minutes, stirring occasionally. Uncover the pan, and cook over medium-high heat for 10–15 minutes, or until onions are lightly browned.
3. Add beans, carrots, celery, garlic, stock, parsley, rosemary, Italian seasoning, bay leaf, and Parmesan rind, if using. Bring to a boil over high heat, then reduce the heat to low, and simmer soup, covered, for 1½–2 hours, or until beans are tender.

4. While soup simmers, bring a large pot of salted water to a boil over high heat. Add pasta and cook according to package directions until al dente. Drain, and set aside.
5. Remove and discard bay leaf and Parmesan rind, if using. Remove ⅔ of solids from the pan with a slotted spoon, and puree in a food processor fitted with the steel blade or in a blender. Be careful not to fill the beaker too full when blending hot ingredients.
6. Stir puree back into soup, and add pasta and remaining ¼ cup olive oil. Season to taste with salt and pepper, and serve immediately, passing grated Parmesan cheese separately.

Note: The soup can be prepared up to 2 days in advance and refrigerated, tightly covered; refrigerate the pasta separately. Reheat it over low heat, covered, until hot, stirring occasionally.

Variation:

- Substitute garbanzo beans for the borlotti beans.

Cuban Black Bean Soup

Garlic and aromatic spices like cumin and coriander add sparkle to this thick and hearty vegetarian soup. Add a tossed salad and some garlic bread, and the meal is complete.

Yield: 4–6 servings | **Active time:** 15 minutes | **Start to finish:** 2 hours, including 1 hour to soak beans

1 pound dried black beans
¼ cup olive oil
1 large onion, peeled and diced
1 green bell pepper, seeds and ribs removed, finely chopped
6 garlic cloves, peeled and minced
1–2 jalapeño or serrano chiles, seeds and ribs removed, finely chopped
2 tablespoons ground cumin
1 tablespoon ground coriander
6 cups Vegetable Stock (recipe on page 25) or purchased stock
¼ cup chopped fresh cilantro
Salt and freshly ground black pepper to taste
Sour cream (optional)
Lime wedges (optional)

1. Rinse beans in a colander and place them in a mixing bowl covered with cold water. Allow beans to soak overnight. Or place beans in a saucepan and bring to a boil over high heat. Boil 1 minute. Turn off the heat, cover the pan, and soak beans for 1 hour. With either soaking method, drain beans, discard soaking water, and begin cooking as soon as possible.
2. Heat oil in a 4-quart saucepan over medium-high heat. Add onion, green bell pepper, garlic, and chiles. Cook, stirring frequently, for 3 minutes, or until onion is translucent. Reduce the heat to low, and stir in cumin and coriander. Cook, stirring constantly, for 1 minute.
3. Add beans and stock, and bring to a boil over high heat, stirring occasionally. Reduce the heat to low, and simmer soup, partially covered, for 1–1¼ hours, or until beans are soft.

4. Remove 2 cups of beans with a slotted spoon, and puree in a food processor fitted with the steel blade or in a blender. Be careful not to fill the beaker too full when blending hot ingredients. Return beans to the soup, stir in cilantro, season to taste with salt and pepper, and serve hot. Top with a dollop of sour cream and serve with lime wedges, if using.

Note: The soup can be made up to 2 days in advance and refrigerated, tightly covered. Reheat it over low heat, covered, until hot, stirring occasionally.

> There's no question that chiles contain potent oils; however, there's no need to wear rubber gloves when handling them. I cut the chiles on a glass plate rather than on my cutting board so the volatile oils do not penetrate. What's most important is that you wash your hands thoroughly after handling chiles.

Provençal Lentil Soup

Lentils are inherently earthy in flavor, and the orange juice and herbs in this recipe enliven that quality of the healthful legumes. A tossed salad and a loaf of garlic bread can complete your meal.

Yield: 4–6 servings | **Active time:** 15 minutes | **Start to finish:** 45 minutes

1½ cups lentils, preferably green lentils
2 tablespoons olive oil
1 large onion, peeled and diced
8 garlic cloves, peeled and minced
1 large carrot, peeled and sliced
7 cups Vegetable Stock (recipe on page 25) or purchased stock
3 tablespoons chopped fresh parsley
1 tablespoon herbes de Provence
1 (14.5-ounce) can diced tomatoes, undrained
½ cup orange juice
2 tablespoons red wine vinegar
Salt and freshly ground black pepper to taste

1. Place lentils in a sieve, and rinse well under cold running water. Set aside.
2. Heat oil in a 4-quart saucepan over medium-high heat. Add onion, garlic, and carrot, and cook, stirring frequently, for 3 minutes, or until onion is translucent. Add lentils, stock, parsley, and herbes de Provence, and bring to a boil over high heat, stirring occasionally.
3. Reduce the heat to low, and cook soup, covered, for 20 minutes, or until lentils are almost tender. Add tomatoes, orange juice, and vinegar, and cook for an additional 10–12 minutes, or until lentils are very soft.
4. Remove ¾ of solids with a slotted spoon, and puree in a food processor fitted with the steel blade or in a blender. Be careful not to fill the beaker too full when blending hot ingredients.
5. Return puree to the pan, season to taste with salt and pepper, and serve immediately.

Note: The soup can be prepared up to 2 days in advance and refrigerated, tightly covered. Reheat it over low heat, covered, until hot, stirring occasionally.

Italian Bread and Tomato Stew *(Pappa al Pomodoro)*

Aromatic with fresh basil, creamy with cheeses, and robust with heart-healthy tomatoes, this thick bread stew is the epitome of Italian comfort food. Serve it with a green salad, and your meal is complete.

Yield: 6–8 servings | **Active time:** 15 minutes | **Start to finish:** 40 minutes

1 (¾-pound) loaf Italian or French bread
3 cups whole milk
¼ cup olive oil
1 large onion, peeled and diced
2 garlic cloves, peeled and chopped
2 (28-ounce) cans diced tomatoes, drained
½ cup firmly packed chopped fresh basil
½ cup grated whole milk mozzarella cheese
½ cup freshly grated Parmesan cheese
Salt and freshly ground black pepper to taste

1. Break or cut bread into 1-inch cubes. Place cubes in a mixing bowl, and add milk, stirring to press all cubes into liquid.
2. Heat olive oil in a 4-quart saucepan over medium-high heat. Add onion and garlic, and cook, stirring frequently, for 3 minutes, or until onion is translucent. Add tomatoes and cook for 10 minutes, stirring occasionally.
3. Add bread mixture and basil to the saucepan, and bring to a boil over medium-high heat, stirring frequently. Reduce the heat to low, and simmer mixture, uncovered, for 15 minutes. Stir in mozzarella and Parmesan, and simmer for 3 minutes, stirring frequently. Season to taste with salt and pepper, and serve immediately.

Note: The dish can be made up to 2 days in advance and refrigerated, tightly covered. Reheat it over low heat, covered, until hot, stirring occasionally.

Variations:

- Substitute fresh oregano or rosemary, chopped, for the basil.
- Substitute 2 tablespoons Italian seasoning and ¼ cup chopped fresh parsley for the basil.

Cajun Red Bean Stew

Red beans and rice is such an important part of Louisiana's culinary culture that famed jazz musician Louis Armstrong used to sign his letters "red beans and ricely yours." Serve this over rice, of course, with a bowl of coleslaw.

Yield: 4–6 servings | **Active time:** 15 minutes | **Start to finish:** 40 minutes

3 tablespoons olive oil
2 medium onions, peeled and chopped
4 garlic cloves, peeled and minced
1 green bell pepper, seeds and ribs removed, finely diced
1 celery rib, rinsed, trimmed, and chopped
1 tablespoon smoked Spanish paprika
1 cup Vegetable Stock (recipe on page 25) or purchased stock
1 (14.5-ounce) can diced tomatoes, undrained
1 (8-ounce) can tomato sauce
2 tablespoons chopped fresh parsley
1 teaspoon dried thyme
1 chipotle chile in adobo sauce, drained and finely chopped
1 bay leaf
2 (15-ounce) cans red kidney beans, drained and rinsed
Salt and freshly ground black pepper to taste
3 cups cooked brown or white rice, hot

1. Heat oil in a large skillet over medium heat. Add onions, garlic, green pepper, and celery, and cook, stirring frequently, for 8–10 minutes, or until green pepper is tender. Add paprika, and cook for 30 seconds.
2. Add stock, tomatoes, tomato sauce, parsley, thyme, chile, bay leaf, and kidney beans. Bring to a boil, and simmer about 10 minutes, stirring frequently, or until the mixture is slightly thickened.
3. Remove and discard bay leaf. Mash ⅓ of bean mixture with a potato masher. Season to taste with salt and pepper, and serve immediately over rice.

Note: The dish can be cooked up to 2 days in advance and refrigerated, tightly covered. Reheat it over low heat, covered, until hot, stirring occasionally.

Variation:

- If you're just an "occasional vegetarian," transform this to a dish with ham. Substitute chicken stock or ham stock, if you have it, for the vegetable stock, and add ½ pound baked ham, cut into ¾-inch dice, to the dish at Step 2.

A can of chipotle chiles in adobo sauce goes a long way. Chances are you use less than a half-dozen chiles in a given recipe. To save the remainder of the can, place a few chiles with a teaspoon of sauce in ice-cube trays. When they're frozen, transfer them to a heavy resealable plastic bag. Be sure to wash the ice-cube tray well.

Black-eyed Pea Stew with Collard Greens

Both black-eyed peas and collard greens owe their parentage to Africa and were brought over by slaves in the seventeenth and eighteenth centuries. The herbs and chiles make this a vibrantly flavored stew; serve it over rice with a bowl of coleslaw.

Yield: 4–6 servings | **Active time:** 15 minutes | **Start to finish:** 2½ hours

- 1½ cups dried black-eyed peas
- 2 tablespoons vegetable oil
- 1 large onion, peeled and chopped
- 2 garlic cloves, peeled and minced
- 6–7 cups Vegetable Stock (recipe on page 25) or purchased stock
- 1 pound collard greens, stemmed, rinsed well, and thinly sliced
- 1 chipotle chile in adobo sauce, finely chopped
- 2 tablespoons chopped fresh parsley
- 1 teaspoon dried thyme
- 1 teaspoon dried sage
- 1 bay leaf
- Salt and freshly ground black pepper to taste
- 3 cups cooked brown or white rice, hot

1. Place black-eyed peas in a sieve, and rinse well under cold running water. Discard any broken black-eyed peas.
2. Heat oil in a 4-quart saucepan over medium-high heat. Add onion and garlic, and cook, stirring frequently, for 3 minutes, or until onion is translucent.
3. Add black-eyed peas, stock, collard greens, chile, parsley, thyme, sage, and bay leaf to the pan, and bring to a boil over high heat. Reduce the heat to low, and simmer beans, covered, for 1½ hours, or until beans are tender but not mushy.
4. Remove and discard bay leaf, season to taste with salt and pepper, and serve immediately over rice.

Note: The dish can be cooked up to 2 days in advance and refrigerated, tightly covered. Reheat it over low heat, covered, until hot, stirring occasionally.

Variation:

- Substitute mustard greens, Swiss chard, or escarole for the collard greens.

This stew, traditionally known as hoppin' John, dates to the colonial era in the Carolinas and is still eaten to bring good luck on New Year's Day. The black-eyed peas, called "pigeon peas" in Africa, were brought over with the slaves in the seventeenth century, and the first recipe for hoppin' John comes from *The Carolina Housewife*, published in 1847.

Curried Lentil Stew

Healthful lentils, called *dal* in Indian cooking, are one of the few dried legumes that need no presoaking, so this flavorful dish is quickly on your dinner table. Serve it over rice, preferably aromatic basmati rice, with a tossed salad.

Yield: 4–6 servings | **Active time:** 15 minutes | **Start to finish:** 55 minutes

- 1½ cups brown lentils
- ¼ cup vegetable oil
- 2 onions, peeled and chopped
- 3 garlic cloves, peeled and minced
- 1 fresh jalapeño or serrano chile, seeds and ribs removed, finely chopped
- 1 tablespoon curry powder
- 1 teaspoon ground cumin
- 1 teaspoon ground coriander
- ½ teaspoon ground ginger
- 2 medium tomatoes, rinsed, cored, seeded, and chopped
- 4 cups Vegetable Stock (recipe on page 25) or purchased stock
- 2 (3-inch) cinnamon sticks
- 3 medium zucchini, rinsed, trimmed, and cut into ½-inch dice
- ¼ cup chopped fresh cilantro
- Salt and freshly ground black pepper to taste
- 3 cups cooked basmati rice, hot

1. Place lentils in a sieve, and rinse well under cold running water. Set aside.
2. Heat oil in a 4-quart saucepan over medium-high heat. Add onion, garlic, and chile pepper, and cook, stirring frequently, for 3 minutes, or until onion is translucent. Stir in curry powder, cumin, coriander, and ginger. Cook, stirring constantly, for 1 minute.
3. Add tomatoes, lentils, stock, and cinnamon sticks to the pan, and bring to a boil over medium-high heat. Reduce the heat to low, and simmer mixture, uncovered, adding more stock, if necessary, to keep ingredients just covered with liquid, for 30–40 minutes, or until lentils are very soft.

4. Remove and discard cinnamon sticks, and add zucchini to the pan. Cover the pan, and cook for 10 minutes, or until zucchini is tender. Stir in cilantro, season to taste with salt and pepper, and serve immediately over rice.

Note: The dish can be cooked up to 2 days in advance and refrigerated, tightly covered. Reheat it over low heat, covered, until hot, stirring occasionally.

Variation:

- Substitute 1 (10-ounce) package frozen leaf spinach, thawed and squeezed well to extract as much liquid as possible, for 1 of the zucchini.

The flavor of most dried herbs and spices is released if they're sautéed with onions or other vegetables over low heat before adding them to a liquid. Curry powder and chili powder, which are both blends of spices, benefit the most from this precooking.

Cajun Vegetable Stew

I adore the vibrant flavors and colors of Cajun cooking, and this thick and hearty vegetable stew—which is on the table fairly quickly—is a perfect example. Serve it over rice, with a tossed salad.

Yield: 4–6 servings | **Active time:** 15 minutes | **Start to finish:** 40 minutes

2 tablespoons vegetable oil
1 medium onion, peeled and chopped
3 garlic cloves, peeled and minced
2 celery ribs, rinsed, trimmed, and diced
1 carrot, peeled and diced
1 tablespoon smoked Spanish paprika
1 (28-ounce) can diced tomatoes, undrained
3/4 pound sweet potatoes, peeled and cut into 3/4-inch cubes
2 tablespoons chopped fresh parsley
1 teaspoon dried thyme
1 bay leaf
1 (15-ounce) can red kidney beans, drained and rinsed
1 cup frozen sliced okra, thawed
1 cup frozen corn kernels, thawed
Salt and hot red pepper sauce to taste
3 cups cooked brown or white rice, hot

1. Heat oil in a 4-quart saucepan over medium-high heat. Add onion, garlic, celery, and carrot. Cook, stirring frequently, for 3 minutes, or until onion is translucent. Stir in paprika, and cook for 1 minute, stirring constantly.
2. Add tomatoes, sweet potatoes, parsley, thyme, and bay leaf. Bring to a boil, stirring occasionally. Reduce the heat to low, cover the pan, and simmer stew for 15–20 minutes, or until sweet potato is tender.
3. Add kidney beans, okra, and corn. Simmer, covered, for an additional 5 minutes. Uncover the pan, increase the heat to medium, and cook for 5 minutes, or until slightly thickened, stirring frequently.
4. Remove and discard bay leaf, and season to taste with salt and hot red pepper sauce. Serve immediately over rice.

Note: The dish can be prepared up to 2 days in advance and refrigerated, tightly covered. Reheat it over low heat, covered, until hot, stirring occasionally; do not let it boil again.

Variation:

- Substitute redskin potatoes for the sweet potatoes, and substitute baby lima beans for the corn.

> Okra is a natural thickening agent, which is why it's used to make traditional gumbo. But when reheating a dish made with okra, do not let it boil again; it will become stringy.

Southwestern Squash and Bean Stew

While dried beans frequently require different cooking times, all canned beans are totally cooked and can be combined in dishes such as this one. This is an incredibly flavorful dish, partially due to the fresh salsa in the sauce. Serve it over hot brown rice.

Yield: 4–6 servings | **Active time:** 15 minutes | **Start to finish:** 35 minutes

3 tablespoons olive oil
1 large onion, peeled and diced
3 garlic cloves, peeled and minced
1 green bell pepper, seeds and ribs removed, finely chopped
2 tablespoons chili powder
1 teaspoon ground cumin
1 teaspoon dried oregano
1 (15-ounce) can tomato sauce
¾ cup refrigerated salsa
¾ cup Vegetable Stock (recipe on page 25) or purchased stock
2 medium yellow squash, rinsed, trimmed, and cut into ½-inch dice
1 (15-ounce) can red kidney beans, drained and rinsed
1 (15-ounce) can garbanzo beans, drained and rinsed
Salt and freshly ground black pepper
3 cups cooked brown or white rice, hot

1. Heat olive oil in a 4-quart saucepan over medium-high heat. Add onion, garlic, and green bell pepper, and cook, stirring frequently, for 3 minutes, or until onion is translucent. Stir in chili powder, cumin, and oregano. Cook for 1 minute, stirring constantly.
2. Stir in tomato sauce, salsa, stock, yellow squash, kidney beans, and garbanzo beans, and bring to a boil. Reduce the heat to low and simmer, uncovered, for 20 minutes, or until squash is tender. Season to taste with salt and pepper, and serve immediately over rice.

Note: The dish can be made up to 2 days in advance and refrigerated, tightly covered. Reheat it over low heat, covered, until hot, stirring occasionally.

Variation:

- Substitute black beans for the kidney and garbanzo beans, and substitute zucchini for the yellow squash.

Mediterranean Vegetable Stew

Like many vegetable stews in this chapter, this one is also delicious served cold as a side dish to accompany any simple grilled or broiled entree. If serving it hot, orzo is a good base, and a tossed salad and the focaccia in Chapter 8 are wonderful with it.

Yield: 4–6 servings | **Active time:** 20 minutes | **Start to finish:** 45 minutes

- 3 tablespoons olive oil
- 1 large onion, peeled and diced
- 3 garlic cloves, peeled and minced
- 1 (28-ounce) can diced tomatoes, undrained
- ½ pound redskin potatoes, scrubbed and cut into 1-inch cubes
- ¼ cup chopped fresh parsley
- 2 teaspoons dried oregano
- 2 small zucchini, rinsed, trimmed, and cut into 1-inch cubes
- ½ pound fresh green beans, rinsed, trimmed, and cut into 1-inch lengths
- Salt and freshly ground black pepper to taste

1. Heat oil in a 4-quart saucepan over medium-high heat. Add onion and garlic, and cook, stirring frequently, for 3 minutes, or until onion is translucent.
2. Add tomatoes, potatoes, parsley, and oregano, and bring to a boil over medium-high heat. Reduce the heat to low, and simmer, covered, for 15 minutes. Add zucchini and green beans, and simmer for an additional 10–12 minutes, or until vegetables are tender.
3. Season to taste with salt and pepper, and serve hot, at room temperature, or chilled.

Note: The dish can be prepared up to 2 days in advance and refrigerated, tightly covered. Reheat it over low heat, covered, until hot, stirring occasionally.

Variation:

- Substitute 1 tablespoon herbes de Provence for the oregano, and add 2 teaspoons grated orange zest and ½ cup dry white wine to the dish.

Greek Ratatouille

Ratatouille is the time-honored French mélange of various vegetables, always including eggplant and tomato. This version—with dill, lemon juice, and oregano—takes on Greek flavors. Serve it on top of orzo, with a crusty bread from Chapter 8.

Yield: 4–6 servings | **Active time:** 25 minutes | **Start to finish:** 1 hour

1 small eggplant, rinsed, trimmed, and cut into 1-inch cubes
¼ cup olive oil, divided
1 medium onion, peeled and diced
3 garlic cloves, peeled and minced
1 green bell pepper, seeds and ribs removed, cut into 1-inch dice
1 (28-ounce) can diced tomatoes, undrained
1 tablespoon tomato paste
1 tablespoon dried oregano
2 medium zucchini, rinsed, trimmed, and cut into 1-inch cubes
1 (10-ounce) package frozen cut green beans, thawed
3 tablespoons lemon juice
3 tablespoons chopped fresh dill
2 tablespoons chopped fresh parsley
Salt and freshly ground black pepper to taste

1. Place eggplant in a colander, and sprinkle cubes liberally with salt. Place a plate on top of eggplant cubes, and weight the plate with some cans. Place the colander in the sink or on a plate, and allow eggplant to drain for 30 minutes. Rinse eggplant cubes, and squeeze hard to remove water. Wring out remaining water with a tea towel.
2. Heat 2 tablespoons oil in a 4-quart saucepan over medium-high heat. Add onion, garlic, and green bell pepper, and cook, stirring frequently, for 3 minutes, or until onion is translucent. Scrape mixture into a mixing bowl.
3. Add remaining 2 tablespoons oil to pan, and cook eggplant for 3–4 minutes, or until lightly browned. Return onion mixture to the pan, and add tomatoes, tomato paste, and oregano. Stir well to dissolve tomato paste.

4. Bring to boil over medium-high heat, then reduce the heat to low, and simmer vegetables, uncovered, for 10 minutes. Add zucchini, and cook for an additional 5 minutes. Add green beans, lemon juice, dill, and parsley. Bring back to a boil and simmer for 3 minutes. Season to taste with salt and pepper, and serve hot, at room temperature, or chilled.

Note: The dish can be prepared up to 2 days in advance and refrigerated, tightly covered. Reheat it, covered, in a 350°F oven for 20–25 minutes, or until hot.

Variation:

- For a classic ratatouille, omit the green beans, oregano, lemon juice, and dill, and add 1 tablespoon herbes de Provence.

When cooking with wine or any other acid such as lemon juice, it's important to use a stainless-steel or coated steel pan rather than aluminum. When mixed with the wine or acid, an aluminum pan can impart a metallic taste to the dish.

Vegetarian Chili with Tofu

This chili preparation is at the delicate side of the spectrum; it contains mild green chiles and requires a restrained hand in the spicing. The cubes of tofu absorb the flavor of the sauce wonderfully.

Yield: 4–6 servings | **Active time:** 20 minutes | **Start to finish:** 2 hours, including 1 hour to soak beans

- 1½ cups dried pinto beans
- 2 tablespoons olive oil
- 2 large onions, peeled and diced
- 2 green bell peppers, seeds and ribs removed, chopped
- 2 garlic cloves, peeled and minced
- 2 tablespoons chili powder
- 1 tablespoon ground cumin
- 1 tablespoon dried oregano
- 1 (28-ounce) can crushed tomatoes in tomato puree
- 1 (4-ounce) can chopped mild green chiles, drained
- 2 tablespoons tomato paste
- 1 cup Vegetable Stock (recipe on page 25) or purchased stock
- 1 (14-ounce) package extra-firm tofu, drained and cut into ¾-inch dice
- Salt and freshly ground black pepper to taste

1. Rinse beans in a colander and place them in a mixing bowl covered with cold water. Allow beans to soak overnight. Or place beans in a saucepan and bring to a boil over high heat. Boil 1 minute. Turn off the heat, cover the pan, and soak beans for 1 hour. With either soaking method, drain beans, discard soaking water, and begin cooking as soon as possible.
2. Heat oil in a 4-quart saucepan over medium-high heat. Add onions, green bell peppers, and garlic, and cook, stirring frequently, for 3 minutes, or until onions are translucent. Add chili powder, cumin, and oregano, and cook, stirring constantly, for 1 minute.
3. Add tomatoes, chiles, tomato paste, and stock. Stir well to dissolve tomato paste. Bring to a boil and cook over low heat, covered, stirring occasionally, for 1 hour. Add tofu, and cook for an additional 15–20 minutes, or until beans are tender. Season to taste with salt and pepper, and serve immediately.

Note: The dish can be prepared up to 2 days in advance and refrigerated, tightly covered. Reheat it over low heat, covered, until hot, stirring occasionally.

Variation:

- Substitute ¾ pound ground turkey for the tofu. Cook it with the onions at the onset of the cooking process.

Here's an easy way to remove the seeds and ribs from bell peppers: Cut a slice off the bottom so the pepper stands up straight. You'll see that there are natural curves to the sections. Holding the pepper by its stem, cut down those curves, and you'll be left with a skeleton of ribs and seeds. Throw it out, and you're ready to chop the peppers.

Tofu Stew with Dried Fruit in Mustard Sauce

Tofu absorbs flavors so wonderfully, and the variety of vegetables and dried fruits in this stew become the stars. Serve it over polenta or buttered egg noodles, with a sweet and sour red cabbage slaw.

Yield: 4–6 servings | **Active time:** 20 minutes | **Start to finish:** 35 minutes

2 (12–14-ounce) packages firm tofu
3 tablespoons vegetable oil
1 large onion, peeled and diced
2 garlic cloves, peeled and minced
1 green bell pepper, seeds and ribs removed, thinly sliced
1 large carrot, peeled and sliced
2 celery ribs, rinsed, trimmed, and sliced
2 cups apple juice
3 tablespoons Dijon mustard
½ cup chopped dried apricots
¼ cup raisins
¼ cup dried cranberries
2 tablespoons chopped fresh parsley
1 teaspoon dried sage
1 tablespoon cornstarch
2 tablespoons cold water
Salt and freshly ground black pepper to taste

1. Drain tofu, cut into 1-inch dice, and set aside.
2. Heat oil in a large, deep skillet over medium-high heat. Add onion and garlic, and cook, stirring frequently, for 3 minutes, or until onion is translucent. Add green bell pepper, carrot, celery, apple juice, mustard, dried apricots, raisins, dried cranberries, parsley, and sage. Bring to a boil, stirring occasionally. Reduce the heat to medium, and simmer for 10 minutes, or until vegetables are almost tender.
3. Add tofu, and cook for 5 minutes. Combine cornstarch and water in a small cup, and add mixture to the skillet. Cook for 1–2 minutes, or until slightly thickened. Season to taste with salt and pepper, and serve immediately.

Note: The dish can be prepared up to 2 days in advance and refrigerated, tightly covered. Reheat it over low heat, covered, until hot, stirring occasionally.

Variation:

- Substitute zucchini or yellow squash, rinsed, trimmed, and cut into 1-inch cubes, for the tofu. Add the zucchini at the onset of cooking with the green bell pepper and carrot.

Dijon mustard, known for its clean, sharp flavor, was actually invented in Dijon, France. It is made from a combination of brown and black mustard seeds, and the essential ingredients are white wine and unfermented grape juice.

Curried Tofu Stew

Healthful broccoli and cauliflower, which retain their texture as well as color, join cubes of springy tofu in a vibrant sauce tempered with lush coconut milk. Serve the stew over fragrant basmati rice.

Yield: 4–6 servings | **Active time:** 20 minutes | **Start to finish:** 25 minutes

2 (12–14-ounce) packages firm tofu
2 tablespoons Asian sesame oil*
1 tablespoon vegetable oil
1 large onion, peeled and diced
1 carrot, peeled and grated
3 garlic cloves, peeled and minced
3 tablespoons curry powder
2 teaspoons ground cumin
1 (14-ounce) can light coconut milk
2 cups broccoli florets
2 cups cauliflower florets
½ cup raisins
Salt and freshly ground black pepper to taste
3 cups cooked basmati rice, hot

1. Drain tofu, cut into 1-inch dice, and set aside.
2. Heat sesame and vegetable oils in a 4-quart saucepan over medium heat. Add onion, carrot, and garlic. Cook, stirring frequently, for 5 minutes, or until onion softens. Stir in curry powder and cumin. Cook for 1 minute, stirring constantly.
3. Add coconut milk, raise the heat to medium-high, and bring to a boil. Add broccoli, cauliflower, tofu, and raisins, and reduce the heat to medium-low. Simmer, uncovered, for 5–7 minutes, or until vegetables are crisp-tender. Season to taste with salt and pepper, and serve immediately with rice.

Note: The dish can be prepared up to 2 days in advance and refrigerated, tightly covered. Reheat it over low heat, covered, until hot, stirring occasionally.

*Available in the Asian aisle of most supermarkets and in specialty markets.

Variation:

- Substitute 2–3 cups diced cooked chicken for the tofu.

While it's a good idea to toss out any dried herb or spice that's been open for more than six months, abbreviate the life of curry powder to two months. This ground blend, composed of up to 20 herbs and spices, loses its flavor and aroma very quickly.

Asian Citrus Tofu Stew

A combination of lemon and orange juice, plus lots of Asian seasoning, makes this a light but satisfying stew. Serve it over aromatic jasmine rice, with some cucumbers and rice vinegar on the side.

Yield: 4–6 servings | **Active time:** 25 minutes | **Start to finish:** 25 minutes

2 (12–14-ounce) packages firm tofu
1 tablespoon cornstarch
2 tablespoons cold water
1 cup orange juice
¼ cup lemon juice
¼ cup granulated sugar
¼ cup soy sauce
2 tablespoons vegetable oil
2 tablespoons Asian sesame oil*
6 scallions, white parts and 4 inches of green tops, rinsed, trimmed, and sliced, divided
3 garlic cloves, peeled and minced
2 tablespoons grated fresh ginger
3 cups sliced bok choy
¼ pound fresh green beans, rinsed, trimmed, and cut into 1-inch lengths
Salt and freshly ground black pepper to taste
3 cups cooked jasmine rice, hot

1. Drain tofu, cut into 1-inch dice, and set aside. Combine cornstarch and cold water in a small bowl, stir well, and set aside. Combine orange juice, lemon juice, sugar, and soy sauce in another small bowl, and set aside.
2. Heat vegetable oil and sesame oil in a wok or heavy skillet over high heat, swirling to coat the pan. Add ½ of scallions, garlic, and ginger, and stir-fry for 30 seconds, or until fragrant. Add bok choy and stir-fry for 1 minute. Add tofu and stir in sauce mixture. Cook for 2 minutes, stirring frequently.

*Available in the Asian aisle of most supermarkets and in specialty markets.

3. Add green beans to the pan, and cook for 1 minute. Stir in cornstarch mixture and cook, stirring constantly, for 1 minute, or until sauce has slightly thickened. Season to taste with salt and pepper. Serve immediately with rice, sprinkling each serving with remaining scallions.

Note: The dish can be prepared up to 2 days in advance and refrigerated, tightly covered. Reheat it over low heat, covered, until hot, stirring occasionally.

Variation:

- Substitute 2–3 cups diced cooked chicken for the tofu.

> Many a cook has suffered a scraped knuckle while grating fresh ginger. If the ginger knob is large, peel only the amount you think you'll need and hold on to the remainder. If you're down to a small part, impale it on a fork and use that as your grating handle.

Chapter 5:

Aquatic Adventures: Soups and Stews with Fish and Seafood

While fish is usually higher in price than most meats, there is no waste to a fish fillet, and with its low fat content, fish doesn't shrink the way that meats do. So the price per edible ounce of fish is really about the same as for other forms of protein, like a chuck roast or pork loin, if still more expensive than a chicken.

"This is a fine kettle of fish" is a phrase I hope you'll use often when cooking the recipes in this chapter. This eighteenth-century expression originally meant "a different situation than one previously mentioned." I hope that these recipes will show you that if you don't think that fish and seafood make wonderful soups and stews, you'll find you're in a different situation.

While chicken and meats are added to the soup and stew base at the onset of cooking, or soon thereafter, fish or seafood is the last ingredient to be added to these recipes, because of its short cooking time. Cubes of fish cook in 3 to 5 minutes, while it can take cubes of beef up to 3 hours to reach tenderness. In fact, overcooking is a common mistake cooks make when handling seafood.

Another difference when cooking fish and seafood is that it does not freeze well—either before or after cooking. The reason is that when food is frozen, the liquid inside the cells expands to form ice. This expansion punctures the delicate cell walls, which makes the fish mushy once thawed.

But the fish cooks quickly! It's the base that takes the time. So my suggestion is to double or even triple the recipe for the base *only.* Then freeze the extra portions of base. Thaw it when you come home, add the fresh fish, and within 10 minutes you'll be enjoying a delicious meal with a long-simmered soup or stew base enlivened by perfectly cooked fish.

In a similar fashion, while all fish soups and stews can be made 1 day in advance and gently reheated, it's almost impossible to reheat cooked mussels. If using mussels, cook the base in advance and then cook the mussels just prior to serving.

I also realize that many people who enjoy fish don't enjoy "fishy" flavor. But there's a way around that for these recipes. Rather than using the seafood stock specified, substitute vegetable or chicken stock. The "fishy" quotient will be greatly diminished.

FISH FACTS

Fish are high in protein and low to moderate in fat, cholesterol, and sodium. A 3-ounce portion of fish has between 47 and 170 calories, depending on the species. Fish are an excellent source of B vitamins, iodine, phosphorus, potassium, iron, and calcium.

The most important nutrient in fish may be the omega-3 fatty acids. These are the primary polyunsaturated fatty acids found in the fat and oils of fish. They have been found to lower levels of low-density lipoproteins (LDL), the "bad" cholesterol, and raise levels of high-density lipoproteins (HDL), the "good" cholesterol. Fatty fish that live in cold water, such as mackerel and salmon, seem to have the most omega-3 fatty acids, although all fish have some.

BOUNTIFUL OPTIONS

It's more important to use the freshest fish—and one that is reasonably priced—than any specific fish; that's why these recipes are not written for cod, halibut, or pompano. They're written for two generic types of fish—thin white-fleshed fillets and thick white-fleshed fish fillets. These encompass the most types of fish.

White-fleshed fish are all low in fat, are mild to delicate in flavor, and flake easily when cooked. The only species of fish that should *not* be used in these recipes are tuna, bluefish, and mackerel; they will all be too strong. Salmon, if you find it at a good price, can be substituted for either classification of fish, depending on the thickness of the fillet.

There are thousands of species that fit these rather large definitions. Here are some of the most common:

- **Thin fillets:** Flounder, sole, perch, red snapper, trout, tilapia, ocean perch, catfish, striped bass, turbot, and whitefish.

- **Thick fillets:** Halibut, scrod, grouper, sea bass, mahi-mahi, pompano, yellowtail, cod, haddock, and swordfish.

SECRETS TO SELECTION

Most supermarkets still display fish on chipped ice in a case rather than pre-packaging it, and they should. Fish should be kept at even a lower temperature than meats. Fish fillets or steaks should look bright, lustrous, and moist, with no signs of discoloration or drying.

When making your fish selection, keep a few simple guidelines in mind: Above all, do not buy any fish that actually smells fishy, indicating that it is no longer fresh or hasn't been cut or stored properly. Fresh fish has the mild, clean scent of the sea—nothing more. Look for bright, shiny colors in the fish scales, because as a fish sits, its skin becomes more pale and dull looking. Then peer into the eyes; they should be black and beady. If they're milky or sunken, the fish has been dead too long. And if the fish isn't behind glass, gently poke its flesh. If the indentation remains, the fish is old.

Rinse all fish under cold running water before cutting or cooking. With fillets, run your fingers in every direction along the top of the fillet before cooking, and feel for any pesky little bones.

You can remove bones easily in two ways. Larger bones will come out if they're stroked with a vegetable peeler, and you can pull out smaller bones with tweezers. This is not a long process, but it's a gesture that will be greatly appreciated by all who eat the fish.

Manhattan Clam Chowder

Adding tomatoes and other vegetables to chowder is heresy in New England, but this version is popular from the mid-Atlantic states south. While named for New York, legend has it that the chowder was actually developed by the Portuguese settlers in Rhode Island.

Yield: 4–6 servings | **Active time:** 30 minutes | **Start to finish:** 45 minutes

2 tablespoons olive oil
1 medium onion, peeled and diced
1 green bell pepper, seeds and ribs removed, diced
2 celery ribs, rinsed, trimmed, and sliced
2 large redskin potatoes, scrubbed and cut into 1/3-inch dice
1 pint fresh minced clams, drained, with juice reserved
2 (8-ounce) bottles clam juice
1 (14.5-ounce) can diced tomatoes, preferably petite diced, undrained
3 tablespoons chopped fresh parsley
1 teaspoon dried thyme
Salt and freshly ground black pepper to taste

1. Heat oil in a heavy 4-quart saucepan over medium-high heat. Add onion, bell pepper, and celery. Cook, stirring frequently, for 3 minutes, or until onion is translucent.
2. Add potatoes, juice from fresh clams, bottled clam juice, tomatoes, parsley, and thyme to the pan. Bring to a boil, reduce the heat to low, and simmer for 10 minutes, or until potatoes are tender, stirring occasionally. Add clams, bring soup back to a boil, and simmer for 5 minutes. Season to taste with salt and pepper, and serve immediately.

Note: The soup can be made up to 2 days in advance and refrigerated, tightly covered. Reheat it over low heat, covered, until hot, stirring occasionally.

Variations:

- To add some Southwestern flavor, substitute 2 tablespoons chili powder, 2 teaspoons ground cumin, and 1 teaspoon dried oregano for the thyme, and substitute chopped cilantro for the parsley.
- Substitute 3/4 pound thin white-fleshed fish fillets, cut into 1/2-inch cubes, for the clams.

New England Clam Chowder

Early chowder recipes call for everything from beer to ketchup, but not milk. What we know as New England chowder dates from the mid-nineteenth century. My version includes celery and herbs, which create a more complex flavor.

Yield: 4–6 servings | **Active time:** 20 minutes | **Start to finish:** 40 minutes

1 pint fresh minced clams
4 tablespoons (½ stick) unsalted butter, divided
2 medium onions, peeled and diced
2 celery ribs, rinsed, trimmed, and diced
1 (8-ounce) bottle clam juice
2 medium redskin potatoes, scrubbed and cut into ½-inch dice
2 tablespoons chopped fresh parsley
1 bay leaf
1 teaspoon dried thyme
Salt and freshly ground black pepper to taste
3 tablespoons all-purpose flour
3 cups whole milk

1. Drain clams in a sieve over a bowl, reserving the juice in the bowl. Press down with the back of a spoon to extract as much liquid as possible from clams.
2. Melt 2 tablespoons butter in a 4-quart saucepan over medium heat. Add onions and celery, and cook, stirring frequently, for 3 minutes, or until onions are translucent. Add bottled clam juice and reserved clam juice to the pan, along with potatoes, parsley, bay leaf, thyme, salt, and pepper. Bring to a boil, reduce the heat to low, and simmer, covered, for 10–12 minutes, or until potatoes are tender.
3. While mixture simmers, melt remaining 2 tablespoons butter in a small saucepan over low heat. Stir in flour and cook, stirring constantly, for 2 minutes. Raise the heat to medium and whisk in milk. Bring to a boil, whisking frequently, and simmer for 2 minutes.
4. Stir thickened milk into the pan with the vegetables, and add clams. Bring to a boil over medium heat, then reduce the heat to low, and simmer, uncovered, for 3 minutes. Remove and discard bay leaf, season to taste with salt and pepper, and serve immediately.

Note: The soup can be made up to 2 days in advance and refrigerated, tightly covered. Reheat it over low heat, covered, until hot, stirring occasionally.

Variations:

- Start by cooking ¼ pound bacon until crisp, and then use 2 tablespoons bacon fat instead of butter to sauté the vegetables. Crumble the bacon and add along with the clams.
- Add 1 cup cooked corn kernels along with the clams.
- Cook ½ green bell pepper, finely chopped, along with the onions.

In Melville's *Moby-Dick*, Ishmael and Queequeg land on Nantucket and are sent to Hosea Hussey's Try Pots; the name comes from the black iron cauldron used aboard whale ships for melting blubber to liquid oil. Melville writes that the "fishiest of all fishy places was the Try Pots. Chowder for breakfast, and chowder for dinner, and chowder for supper."

Spicy Southern Fish Soup

This tomato-based soup is flavored with herbs and lots of hot red pepper sauce in the Southern tradition. Serve it with cornbread or biscuits, and a tossed green salad.

Yield: 4–6 servings | **Active time:** 15 minutes | **Start to finish:** 40 minutes

3 tablespoons olive oil
2 medium onions, peeled and diced
1 green bell pepper, seeds and ribs removed, chopped
2 celery ribs, rinsed, trimmed, and diced
½ cup dry white wine
2 cups Seafood Stock (recipe on page 26) or purchased stock
3½ cups tomato juice
1 pound redskin potatoes, scrubbed and cut into ¾-inch dice
3 tablespoons chopped fresh parsley
1 teaspoon hot red pepper sauce, or to taste
1½ teaspoons dried oregano
½ teaspoon dried thyme
1 bay leaf
2 (10-ounce) packages frozen mixed vegetables, thawed
1¼ pounds thick white firm-fleshed fish fillets, rinsed and cut into 1-inch cubes
Salt and freshly ground black pepper to taste

1. Heat oil in a 4-quart saucepan over medium-high heat. Add onion, green bell pepper, and celery, and cook, stirring frequently, for 3 minutes, or until onions are translucent. Add wine, and cook for 3 minutes.
2. Add stock, tomato juice, potatoes, parsley, hot red pepper sauce, oregano, thyme, and bay leaf to the pan. Bring to a boil over high heat, then reduce the heat to low, and simmer soup, partially covered, for 12–15 minutes, or until potatoes are tender.
3. Add mixed vegetables to the pan, and cook for 5 minutes. Add fish to the pan, and cook for 3–5 minutes, or until fish is cooked through and flakes easily. Remove and discard bay leaf, season to taste with salt and pepper, and serve immediately.

Note: The soup can be prepared up to 2 days in advance and refrigerated, tightly covered. Reheat it over low heat, covered, until hot, stirring occasionally.

Variation:

- Cook 4 slices bacon, cut into 1-inch sections, in a skillet over medium-high heat for 5–7 minutes, or until crisp. Remove bacon from the skillet with a slotted spoon, and set aside. Discard all but 3 tablespoons bacon fat from the skillet, and use bacon fat instead of oil for sautéing vegetables. Sprinkle bacon on top of fish before serving.

If you're not worrying about cholesterol, always save your bacon fat and use it for cooking. It's free; you've already bought (and eaten) the bacon. It also adds a smoky nuance to dishes.

Bahamian Fish Soup

The islands of the Caribbean have produced many delicious fish soups and stews, including this one. It's spiked with rum and allspice to add those tropical flavors. Serve it over rice or serve some cornbread along with it.

Yield: 4–6 servings | **Active time:** 15 minutes | **Start to finish:** 45 minutes

3 tablespoons olive oil
1 large onion, peeled and diced
1 green bell pepper, seeds and ribs removed, chopped
2 carrots, peeled and diced
2 celery ribs, rinsed, trimmed, and diced
3 garlic cloves, peeled and minced
6 cups Seafood Stock (recipe on page 26) or purchased stock
2 tablespoons tomato paste
2 tablespoons Worcestershire sauce
2 tablespoons rum
3 tablespoons chopped fresh cilantro
1 teaspoon dried thyme
½ teaspoon ground allspice
½ teaspoon hot red pepper sauce, or to taste
1 bay leaf
1¼ pounds thick white firm-fleshed fish fillets, rinsed and cut into 1-inch cubes
Salt and freshly ground black pepper to taste
3 cups cooked brown or white rice, hot

1. Heat oil in a 4-quart saucepan over medium-high heat. Add onion, green bell pepper, carrots, celery, and garlic. Cook, stirring frequently, for 3 minutes, or until onion is translucent.
2. Add stock and tomato paste, and stir well to dissolve tomato paste. Add Worcestershire sauce, rum, cilantro, thyme, allspice, hot red pepper sauce, and bay leaf. Bring to a boil, stirring occasionally.
3. Reduce the heat to low, and simmer soup, partially covered, for 15–20 minutes, or until vegetables are tender. Add fish, cover the pan again, and cook for 3–5 minutes, or until fish is cooked and flakes easily. Remove and discard bay leaf, season to taste with salt and pepper, and serve immediately over rice.

Note: The soup can be prepared up to 1 day in advance and refrigerated, tightly covered. Reheat it over low heat, covered, until hot, stirring occasionally.

Variation:

- Substitute chicken stock for the seafood stock, and substitute 2–3 cups diced cooked chicken for the fish.

> Allspice got its name because its flavor and aroma are reminiscent of a combination of cinnamon, nutmeg, and cloves. If you don't have allspice around, use a pinch of each of those spices to replicate the flavor.

Seafood Minestrone with Herb Oil

This hearty soup contains the large variety of vegetables found in other Italian minestrone soups. But the herb oil drizzled over it before serving adds both aroma and flavor. Serve it with a crusty loaf of garlic bread.

Yield: 4–6 servings | **Active time:** 25 minutes | **Start to finish:** 50 minutes

SOUP

- 1/4 pound small shells or other small pasta
- 3 tablespoons olive oil
- 1 large onion, peeled and diced
- 2 garlic cloves, peeled and minced
- 1 large carrot, peeled and sliced
- 1/2 fennel bulb, rinsed, trimmed, and diced
- 2 cups shredded green cabbage
- 5 cups Seafood Stock (recipe on page 26) or purchased stock
- 1 (14.5-ounce) can diced tomatoes, undrained
- 2 tablespoons chopped fresh parsley
- 1 teaspoon dried oregano
- 1/2 teaspoon dried thyme
- 1 bay leaf
- 1 medium zucchini, rinsed, trimmed, and diced
- 1 cup canned white cannellini beans, drained and rinsed
- 1 pound thick white firm-fleshed fish fillets, rinsed and cut into 1-inch cubes
- Salt and freshly ground black pepper to taste
- 1/2 cup freshly grated Parmesan cheese

HERB OIL

- 3/4 cup firmly packed fresh parsley leaves
- 2 garlic cloves, peeled and minced
- 2 teaspoons Italian seasoning
- 1/3 cup olive oil
- Salt and freshly ground black pepper to taste

1. Bring a large pot of salted water to a boil. Add pasta and cook according to package directions until al dente. Drain, and set aside.
2. While pasta is cooking, heat olive oil in a 4-quart saucepan over medium-high heat. Add onion, garlic, carrot, fennel, and cabbage. Cook, stirring frequently, for 3 minutes, or until onion is translucent. Add stock, tomatoes, parsley, oregano, thyme, and bay leaf. Bring to a boil over high heat, stirring occasionally.
3. Reduce the heat to low, and simmer soup, partially covered, for 10 minutes. Add zucchini and beans, and cook for 5–7 minutes, or until vegetables are almost tender. Add fish, cover the pan, and cook for 3–5 minutes, or until fish is cooked and flakes easily. Remove and discard bay leaf, add pasta, and season to taste with salt and pepper.
4. While soup simmers, prepare herb oil. Combine parsley, garlic, Italian seasoning, and oil in a food processor fitted with the steel blade or in a blender. Be careful not to fill the beaker too full when blending hot ingredients. Puree until smooth. Season to taste with salt and pepper, and scrape mixture into a bowl.
5. To serve, ladle soup into bowls, and pass herb oil and Parmesan cheese separately.

Note: The soup can be prepared up to 1 day in advance and refrigerated, tightly covered. Reheat it over low heat, covered, until hot, stirring occasionally.

Variation:

- Substitute 4 (5-ounce) cans light tuna, drained, for the fish.

> Fresh fennel, sometimes called "anise" in supermarkets, has a slight licorice taste but the texture of celery—both raw and cooked. You can always substitute 2 celery ribs for each ½ fennel bulb specified in a recipe.

Egg Drop Fish Soup

The vegetables in this Asian-inspired soup remain crisp, and the eggs are an easy way to include more protein, too. Serve it over rice, with some cucumbers marinated in rice vinegar on the side.

Yield: 4–6 servings | **Active time:** 20 minutes | **Start to finish:** 35 minutes

6 scallions, white parts and 4 inches of green tops, rinsed and trimmed
7 cups Seafood Stock (recipe on page 26) or purchased stock
1⁄4 cup soy sauce
3 garlic cloves, peeled and minced
1 tablespoon grated fresh ginger
1 large carrot, peeled and shredded
1 celery rib, rinsed, trimmed, and shredded
1⁄4 pound mushrooms, wiped with a damp paper towel, trimmed, and thinly sliced
1 (8-ounce) can water chestnuts, rinsed and diced*
1 cup sliced bok choy
1⁄4 pound green beans, rinsed, trimmed, and cut into 1⁄2-inch slices on the diagonal
11⁄2 tablespoons cornstarch
2 tablespoons cold water
2 large eggs, lightly beaten
2 tablespoons Asian sesame oil*
1 pound thick white firm-fleshed fish fillets, rinsed and cut into 1-inch cubes
Salt and freshly ground black pepper to taste
3 cups cooked brown or white rice, hot

1. Slice scallions, keeping white parts and green tops separate.
2. Combine white parts of scallions, stock, soy sauce, garlic, ginger, carrot, celery, and mushrooms in a 4-quart saucepan, and bring to a boil over high heat, stirring occasionally. Reduce the heat to low, and simmer soup, uncovered, for 5 minutes. Add water chestnuts, bok choy, and green beans, and bring back to a boil. Simmer for 2 minutes.

*Available in the Asian aisle of most supermarkets and in specialty markets.

3. Combine cornstarch and cold water in a small cup. Add to soup, and cook for 2 minutes, or until slightly thickened. Slowly add eggs while stirring. Simmer 1 minute, and stir in sesame oil.
4. Add fish, cover the pan, and cook for 3–5 minutes, or until fish is cooked and flakes easily. Season to taste with salt and pepper, and serve immediately, garnishing each serving with sliced scallion greens.

Note: The soup can be prepared up to 1 day in advance and refrigerated, tightly covered. Reheat it over low heat, covered, until hot, stirring occasionally.

Variation:

- Substitute chicken stock for the seafood stock, and add 2–3 cups cooked diced chicken instead of the fish.

Green beans are a wonderful substitute for very pricey snow peas in the cost-busting kitchen. They offer the same green color and delicate crunchy flavor, but at a far lower cost. They do, however, require a slightly longer cooking time. Snow peas are usually cooked for merely 30–45 seconds, and green beans should be cooked for 1½–2 minutes.

Creamy Tarragon Fish Stew

Aromatic tarragon is one of the herbs used frequently in French cooking, especially with creamed dishes. It has a mild anise flavor, and goes very well with fish. Serve this stew with a tossed green salad.

Yield: 4–6 servings | **Active time:** 20 minutes | **Start to finish:** 45 minutes

- 4 tablespoons (1/2 stick) unsalted butter, divided
- 1 medium onion, peeled and diced
- 2 carrots, peeled and thinly sliced
- 3/4 pound redskin potatoes, scrubbed and cut into 3/4-inch dice
- 1 1/2 cups Seafood Stock (recipe on page 26) or purchased stock
- 1/2 cup dry white wine
- 1 bay leaf
- 3 tablespoons all-purpose flour
- 1 1/2 cups half-and-half or whole milk
- 2 tablespoons chopped fresh parsley
- 2 teaspoons dried tarragon
- Salt and freshly ground black pepper to taste
- 1 pound thick white firm-fleshed fish fillets, cut into 1-inch cubes
- 1 cup frozen peas, thawed

1. Melt 2 tablespoons butter in a saucepan over medium-high heat. Add onion and cook, stirring frequently, for 3 minutes, or until onion is translucent. Add carrots, potatoes, stock, wine, and bay leaf to pan. Bring to a boil, then reduce the heat to low and cook vegetables, uncovered, for 10 minutes, or until potatoes are almost tender. Remove and discard bay leaf. Strain vegetables, and place them in a mixing bowl. Reserve cooking liquid.
2. Melt remaining 2 tablespoons butter in the pan, and stir in flour. Cook over low heat, stirring constantly, for 2 minutes. Whisk in reserved cooking liquid, half-and-half, parsley, and tarragon. Bring to a boil, whisking constantly, and simmer sauce for 2 minutes. Season to taste with salt and pepper.
3. Return vegetables to sauce, and add fish and peas. Bring to a boil over medium heat, then reduce the heat to low, cover the pan, and cook for 3–5 minutes, or until fish is cooked through and flakes easily. Season to taste with salt and pepper, and serve immediately.

Note: The dish can be prepared up to 1 day in advance and refrigerated, tightly covered. Reheat it over low heat, covered, until hot, stirring occasionally.

Variations:

- Substitute 1 pound cooked chicken or turkey for the fish, and substitute chicken stock for the seafood stock.
- Substitute 4 (5-ounce) cans tuna, drained and broken into chunks, for the fish.

> When you're peeling just a few carrots, it makes sense to use a vegetable peeler, or scrub them well and forget about peeling them. If you're doing a lot of carrots, you can pour boiling water over them, and allow them to sit for 5 minutes. The peels will slip right off.

North Beach Cioppino

Cioppino is San Francisco's answer to French bouillabaisse; it's a fish stew made in a richly flavored tomato sauce. I serve it over thick slices of toast, and a green salad is perfect as a foil.

Yield: 4–6 servings | **Active time:** 25 minutes | **Start to finish:** 55 minutes

- 1 pound live mussels
- 3 tablespoons olive oil
- 1 medium onion, peeled and diced
- 3 garlic cloves, peeled and minced
- 1 small fennel bulb, rinsed, trimmed, cored, and diced
- 1 cup dry red wine
- 1½ cups Seafood Stock (recipe on page 26) or purchased stock
- 1 (28-ounce) can crushed tomatoes in tomato puree
- 2 tablespoons chopped fresh parsley
- 1 teaspoon dried thyme
- 1 bay leaf
- ½ teaspoon crushed red pepper flakes, or to taste
- 1 pound thick white firm-fleshed fish fillets, rinsed and cut into 1-inch cubes
- Salt and freshly ground black pepper to taste

1. Just before cooking, clean mussels by scrubbing them well with a brush under cold water; discard any that do not shut tightly. Scrape off any barnacles with a knife. If beard is still attached, remove it by pulling it from tip to hinge or by pulling and cutting it off with knife. Set aside.
2. Heat oil in a 4-quart saucepan over medium-high heat. Add onion, garlic, and fennel, and cook, stirring frequently, for 3 minutes, or until onion is translucent. Add wine, and cook for 3 minutes.
3. Add stock, tomatoes, parsley, thyme, bay leaf, and crushed red pepper flakes. Bring to a boil over medium-high heat, stirring occasionally. Reduce the heat to low, and simmer soup, covered, for 15–20 minutes, or until vegetables soften.
4. Add mussels to the pan, cover the pan, and bring to a boil over high heat. Steam mussels for 3 minutes, and stir to redistribute seafood. Add fish, cover the pan again, and cook for 3–5 minutes, or until fish is cooked and flakes easily. Discard any mussels that did not open.

5. Remove and discard bay leaf, and season to taste with salt and pepper. Serve immediately.

Note: The soup base can be prepared up to 2 days in advance and refrigerated, tightly covered. Reheat it, covered, over low heat, stirring frequently until it comes to a boil, and then add mussels and cook fish.

Variation:

- Substitute white wine for the red wine, and substitute ½ cup orange juice for ½ cup of the seafood stock.

> While the green stalks attached to the fennel bulb aren't used in cooking, there's no reason to discard them. Use them as a substitute for celery to add crunch to salads. They have more flavor than celery, too.

Seafood Gumbo

Gumbo is a classic dish from the Louisiana bayous; the name comes from the African word for "okra," which is used as the thickening agent. This version is only mildly spicy, but feel free to add more hot red pepper sauce if you like fiery flavors. Serve it over rice, with a tossed salad and some cornbread as accompaniments.

Yield: 6–8 servings | **Active time:** 15 minutes | **Start to finish:** 1 hour

- 1/2 cup vegetable oil
- 3/4 cup all-purpose flour
- 2 tablespoons unsalted butter
- 1 large onion, peeled and diced
- 1 large green bell pepper, seeds and ribs removed, diced
- 2 celery ribs, rinsed, trimmed, and diced
- 5 garlic cloves, peeled and minced
- 4 cups Seafood Stock (recipe on page 26) or purchased stock
- 1 teaspoon dried thyme
- 2 bay leaves
- 1 (14.5-ounce) can diced tomatoes, undrained
- 1/2 teaspoon hot red pepper sauce, or to taste
- 1 (1-pound) bag frozen sliced okra, thawed
- 1 1/2 pounds thick white firm-fleshed fish fillets, rinsed and cut into 3/4-inch cubes
- 3 tablespoons chopped fresh parsley
- Salt and freshly ground black pepper to taste
- 3 cups cooked brown or white rice, hot

1. Preheat the oven to 450°F. Combine oil and flour in a Dutch oven, and place the pan in the oven. Bake roux for 20–30 minutes, or until walnut brown, stirring occasionally.
2. While roux bakes, heat butter in large skillet over medium-high heat. Add onion, green pepper, celery, and garlic. Cook, stirring frequently, for 3 minutes, or until onion is translucent. Set aside.
3. Remove roux from the oven, and place the pan on the stove over medium heat. Add stock, and whisk constantly until mixture comes to a boil and thickens. Add vegetable mixture, thyme, bay leaves, tomatoes, and hot red pepper sauce to the pan. Bring to a boil, and cook, covered, over low heat for 20 minutes, stirring occasionally. Add okra, and cook for an additional 10 minutes, or until okra is very tender.

4. Add fish and parsley. Bring back to a boil and cook, covered, over low heat for 3–5 minutes, or until fish is cooked through and flakes easily. Remove and discard bay leaves, season to taste with salt and pepper, and serve immediately over rice.

Note: The soup can be prepared up to 2 days in advance and refrigerated, tightly covered. Reheat it over low heat, covered, until hot, stirring occasionally.

Variations:

- Substitute ½ pound andouille or other spicy sausage for ½ pound of the fish. Brown sausage with the vegetables, and add it to the gumbo along with the stock.
- Transform this recipe into Chicken Gumbo by substituting 1¼ pounds boneless, skinless chicken thighs, cut into 1-inch pieces, for the fish, and chicken stock for the seafood stock. Add chicken to the dish at the onset of the cooking in Step 3.

Roux, pronounced *roo*, as in "kangaroo," is a mixture of fat and flour used as a thickening agent for soups and sauces. The first step in making all roux is to cook the flour, so that the dish doesn't taste like library paste. For white sauces, this is done over low heat and the fat used is butter. Many Creole and Cajun dishes, such as gumbo, use a fuller-flavored brown roux made with oil or drippings and cooked until deep brown. The dark roux gives dishes an almost nutty flavor.

Creole Fish Stew

This is a dish I serve a lot in the summer because it's as good at room temperature as it is hot. It has all the flavors of Louisiana, and it is very easy to make. Serve it with biscuits or cornbread, and a bowl of coleslaw.

Yield: 4–6 servings | **Active time:** 15 minutes | **Start to finish:** 30 minutes

3 tablespoons olive oil
1 large onion, peeled and finely chopped
2 celery ribs, rinsed, trimmed, and finely chopped
3 garlic cloves, peeled and minced
1 green bell pepper, seeds and ribs removed, finely chopped
½ cup Seafood Stock (recipe on page 26) or purchased stock
½ cup dry white wine
1 (14.5-ounce) can diced tomatoes, undrained
1 (15-ounce) can tomato sauce
¼ cup chopped fresh parsley
½ teaspoon dried thyme
1 bay leaf
1½ pounds thick white firm-fleshed fish fillets, rinsed and cut into 1-inch cubes
Salt and hot red pepper sauce to taste

1. Heat oil in a large skillet over medium-high heat. Add onions, celery, garlic, and green bell pepper. Cook, stirring frequently, for 3 minutes, or until onion is translucent. Add stock, wine, tomatoes, tomato sauce, parsley, thyme, and bay leaf. Bring to a boil, reduce the heat to medium, and simmer sauce, uncovered, for 10 minutes, or until reduced by ⅓.
2. Add fish to the skillet. Bring to a boil over medium heat, then reduce the heat to low, cover the pan, and cook for 3–5 minutes, or until fish is cooked through and flakes easily. Remove and discard bay leaf, season to taste with salt and hot red pepper sauce, and serve immediately.

Note: The dish can be prepared up to 1 day in advance and refrigerated, tightly covered. Reheat it over low heat, covered, until hot, stirring occasionally.

Variations:

- Substitute 1½ pounds boneless, skinless chicken breast, cut into 1-inch cubes, for the fish, and substitute chicken stock for the seafood stock. Brown chicken pieces in the oil before cooking the vegetables, and cook chicken, covered, for 10–15 minutes, or until cooked through and no longer pink.
- Substitute 4–6 (½-inch) slices boneless pork loin for the fish, and substitute chicken stock for the seafood stock. Brown pork in the oil before cooking the vegetables, and cook pork for 15–20 minutes, or until cooked through and tender.

While spicier Cajun cooking is native to the Louisiana bayous, Creole cooking was spawned in the grand homes and restaurants of New Orleans. Onion, celery, and green bell peppers is such a popular combination for Creole dishes that it is referred to as the "Holy Trinity of Creole cooking."

Spicy Southwest Fish with Pinto Beans

Mexico has a long coastline on both shores, and this dish is inspired by some authentic preparations from Veracruz. It's made with canned beans, so it's on the table in minutes, and is perfect served with white rice and a tossed salad.

Yield: 4–6 servings | **Active time:** 15 minutes | **Start to finish:** 30 minutes

2 tablespoons olive oil
2 medium onions, peeled and diced
5 garlic cloves, peeled and minced
2 jalapeño or serrano chiles, seeds and ribs removed, finely chopped
1 tablespoon ground cumin
1 (14.5-ounce) can diced tomatoes, drained
2 (15-ounce) cans pinto beans, drained and rinsed
1½ cups Seafood Stock (recipe on page 26) or purchased stock
3 tablespoons chopped fresh cilantro
½ teaspoon dried thyme
1 pound thick white firm-fleshed fish fillets, cut into 1-inch cubes
Salt and freshly ground black pepper to taste
3 cups cooked brown or white rice, hot

1. Heat oil in a large saucepan over medium-high heat. Add onion, garlic, and chiles, and cook, stirring frequently, for 3 minutes, or until onions are translucent. Add cumin, and cook for 1 minute, stirring constantly.
2. Add tomatoes, beans, stock, cilantro, and thyme to the pan. Bring to a boil, reduce the heat to low, and simmer for 10 minutes. Add fish to the pan, and cook for 3–5 minutes, or until fish is cooked through and flakes easily. Season to taste with salt and pepper, and serve immediately.

Note: The dish can be prepared 1 day in advance and refrigerated, tightly covered. Reheat it over low heat, covered, until hot, stirring occasionally.

Variations:

- To make this a vegetarian dish, substitute 1-inch cubes of firm tofu for the fish, and use vegetable stock in the bean mixture.
- Substitute 1-inch cubes of boneless chicken for the fish, and substitute chicken stock for the seafood stock. Cook chicken for 12–15 minutes, or until cooked through and no longer pink.

When cooking hot chiles, be careful that the steam from the pan doesn't get in your eyes. The potent oils in the peppers can be transmitted in the vapor.

Mexican Fish Stew

Most of Mexico is surrounded by either the Pacific Ocean or the Gulf of Mexico, so it should come as no surprise that the cuisine includes many wonderful fish stews. This one has some wonderful garnishes, too.

Yield: 4–6 servings | **Active time:** 20 minutes | **Start to finish:** 55 minutes

STEW

2 tablespoons olive oil
1 medium onion, peeled and diced
½ green bell pepper, seeds and ribs removed, chopped
1 carrot, peeled and diced
1 celery rib, rinsed, trimmed, and diced
2 garlic cloves, peeled and minced
1 small jalapeño or serrano chile, seeds and ribs removed, finely chopped
2 tablespoons chili powder
2 teaspoons ground cumin
1 teaspoon dried oregano
½ cup dry white wine
1½ cups Seafood Stock (recipe on page 26) or purchased stock
1 (28-ounce) can diced tomatoes, undrained
2 tablespoons tomato paste
1 tablespoon granulated sugar
1 bay leaf
1 pound thick white firm-fleshed fish fillets, rinsed and cut into 1-inch cubes
Salt and freshly ground black pepper to taste

GARNISH

3–4 (6-inch) corn tortillas
Vegetable oil spray
½ cup grated Monterey Jack cheese
¼ cup chopped fresh cilantro
4–6 lime wedges

1. Heat oil in a 4-quart saucepan over medium-high heat. Add onion, green bell pepper, carrot, celery, garlic, and chile pepper. Cook, stirring frequently, for 3 minutes, or until onion is translucent. Add chili powder, cumin, and oregano, and cook for 1 minute, stirring constantly. Add wine, and cook for 1 minute.
2. Add stock, tomatoes, tomato paste, sugar, and bay leaf, and stir well to dissolve tomato paste. Bring to a boil over medium-high heat, stirring occasionally.
3. Reduce the heat to low, and simmer soup, covered, for 25 minutes, or until vegetables are soft. Add fish, cover the pan again, and cook for 3–5 minutes, or until fish is cooked through and flakes easily. Remove and discard bay leaf, and season to taste with salt and pepper.
4. While soup simmers, prepare tortilla strips. Preheat the oven to 375°F, line a baking sheet with heavy-duty aluminum foil, and grease the foil with vegetable oil spray. Cut tortillas into ½-inch-wide strips, and arrange strips on the prepared baking sheet. Spray tops of strips with vegetable oil spray. Bake strips for 5–7 minutes, or until crisp. Remove the baking sheet from the oven, and set aside.
5. To serve, ladle soup into bowls, and garnish each serving with tortilla strips, cheese, cilantro, and lime. Serve immediately.

Note: The soup can be prepared up to 1 day in advance and refrigerated, tightly covered. Reheat it over low heat, covered, until hot, stirring occasionally. The tortilla strips can be made up to 2 days in advance and kept at room temperature.

Variation:

- Substitute 3 pounds live mussels for the fish. Just before cooking, clean mussels by scrubbing them well with a brush under cold water; discard any that do not shut tightly. Scrape off any barnacles with a knife. If beard is still attached, remove it by pulling it from tip to hinge or by pulling and cutting it off with knife. Add mussels to the pan, cover the pan, and bring to a boil over high heat. Steam mussels for 3 minutes, stir to redistribute seafood, and steam for an additional 2–3 minutes, or until mussels open. Discard any mussels that do not open.

Italian Mussel Stew with Beans

From Tuscany, this blend of briny mussels, white beans, tomatoes, and lots of garlic makes an ideal supper with a loaf of crusty bread and a green salad.

Yield: 4–6 servings | **Active time:** 20 minutes | **Start to finish:** 50 minutes

- 3 pounds live mussels
- 2 tablespoons olive oil
- 1 large onion, peeled and diced
- 4 garlic cloves, peeled and minced
- 1 large carrot, peeled and diced
- 2 celery ribs, rinsed, trimmed, and diced
- 5 cups Seafood Stock (recipe on page 26) or purchased stock
- 1 (14.5-ounce) can diced tomatoes, undrained
- 1 cup dry white wine
- 3 tablespoons chopped fresh parsley
- 1 teaspoon Italian seasoning
- ½ teaspoon crushed red pepper flakes
- 2 (15-ounce) cans cannellini beans, rinsed and drained
- Salt and freshly ground black pepper to taste

1. Just before cooking, clean mussels by scrubbing them well with a brush under cold water; discard any that do not shut tightly. Scrape off any barnacles with a knife. If beard is still attached, remove it by pulling it from tip to hinge or by pulling and cutting it off with a knife. Set aside.
2. Heat oil in a 4-quart saucepan over medium-high heat. Add onion, garlic, carrot, and celery. Cook, stirring frequently, for 3 minutes, or until onion is translucent. Add stock, tomatoes, wine, parsley, Italian seasoning, and red pepper flakes. Bring to a boil over medium-high heat, stirring occasionally. Reduce the heat to low, and cook, uncovered, for 10 minutes. Add beans, and cook for an additional 5 minutes, or until vegetables are tender.
3. Add mussels to the pan, cover the pan, and bring to a boil over high heat. Steam mussels for 3 minutes, stir to redistribute seafood, and steam for an additional 2–3 minutes, or until mussels open. Discard any mussels that did not open, and remove the pan from the heat.

4. Season broth to taste with salt and pepper. To serve, place mussels in shallow bowls and ladle broth and vegetables on top. Serve with soupspoons as well as seafood forks.

Note: The stew base can be prepared up to 2 days in advance and refrigerated, tightly covered. Reheat it, covered, over low heat, stirring frequently until it comes to a boil, and then add mussels.

Variations:

- Substitute 1¼ pounds thick white firm-fleshed fish fillets, rinsed and cut into 1-inch cubes, for the mussels. Cook the fish for 3–5 minutes, or until it is cooked through and flakes easily.
- Substitute chicken stock for the seafood stock, and substitute 1¼ pounds boneless, skinless chicken breast, cut into 1-inch cubes, for the fish. Add chicken at the onset of the cooking time.

Wines in 3-liter boxes have really improved in quality in recent years. They are great for cooking because the wine never comes into contact with oxygen, which causes it to spoil. That also means that you don't have to refrigerate the wine.

Curried Fish Stew

The curry and chile are tamed by creamy coconut milk in this Indian-inspired fish stew. There are potatoes in the stew, so all you need to complete the meal is a steamed green vegetable or a tossed salad.

Yield: 4–6 servings | **Active time:** 20 minutes | **Start to finish:** 45 minutes

- 2 tablespoons vegetable oil
- 1 small onion, peeled and chopped
- 4 garlic cloves, peeled and minced
- 2 jalapeño or serrano chiles, seeds and ribs removed, chopped
- 3 tablespoons curry powder
- ½ teaspoon ground cinnamon
- Pinch of ground allspice
- ½ cup Seafood Stock (recipe on page 26) or purchased stock
- 3 tablespoons peanut butter
- 1 (15-ounce) can light coconut milk
- 1 teaspoon granulated sugar
- 1 pound redskin potatoes, scrubbed and cut into ¾-inch dice
- 2 carrots, peeled and sliced
- 1¼ pounds thick white firm-fleshed fish fillets, rinsed and cut into 1-inch cubes
- Salt and freshly ground black pepper to taste
- ¼ cup chopped fresh cilantro

1. Heat oil in a deep skillet over medium-high heat. Add onion, garlic, and chiles, and cook, stirring frequently, for 3 minutes, or until onion is translucent. Add curry powder, cinnamon, and allspice, and cook for 1 minute, stirring constantly. Scrape mixture into a food processor fitted with the steel blade or into a blender. Be careful not to fill the beaker too full when blending hot ingredients. Add stock and peanut butter, and puree until smooth.
2. Return puree to the skillet, and add coconut milk and sugar. Bring to a boil over medium-high heat, stirring occasionally. Add potatoes and carrots, and bring to a boil. Reduce the heat to low, cover the pan, and simmer for 12–15 minutes, or until vegetables are tender.
3. Add fish to the pan, and cook for 3–5 minutes, or until fish is cooked through and flakes easily. Season to taste with salt and pepper, and serve immediately, sprinkling each serving with cilantro.

Note: The dish can be prepared up to 1 day in advance and refrigerated, tightly covered. Reheat it over low heat, covered, until hot, stirring occasionally.

Variation:

- Substitute chicken stock for the seafood stock, and substitute 1¼ pounds boneless, skinless chicken breast, cut into 1-inch cubes, for the fish. Add the chicken to the stew along with the potatoes and carrots.

> You'll notice that I specify light coconut milk in recipes—I do this purely for the lower caloric content. I truly cannot taste the difference between full fat coconut milk and the light version which has ⅓ the calories.

Chinese Sweet and Sour Fish Stew

Asian flavors like tangy ginger and aromatic sesame oil add nuances to the traditional sweet and sour flavors of this delicate fish stew. Serve it over rice, preferably aromatic jasmine rice.

Yield: 4–6 servings | **Active time:** 20 minutes | **Start to finish:** 50 minutes

2 tablespoons Asian sesame oil*
1 large onion, peeled, halved, and sliced
4 garlic cloves, peeled and minced
2 tablespoons grated fresh ginger
2 cups Seafood Stock (recipe on page 26) or purchased stock
1/4 cup cider vinegar
1/4 cup firmly packed dark brown sugar
2 tablespoons soy sauce
1 teaspoon Chinese chile paste with garlic*
2 celery ribs, rinsed, trimmed, and sliced
2 carrots, peeled and thinly sliced
2 cups firmly packed sliced green cabbage
1 1/4 pounds thick white firm-fleshed fish fillets, rinsed and cut into 1-inch cubes
1 cup frozen cut green beans, thawed
1 tablespoon cornstarch
2 tablespoons cold water
Salt and crushed red pepper flakes to taste
3 cups cooked brown or white rice, hot

1. Heat oil in a 4-quart saucepan over medium-high heat. Add onion, garlic, and ginger. Cook, stirring frequently, for 3 minutes, or until onion is translucent.
2. Add stock, vinegar, brown sugar, soy sauce, and chile paste to the pan, and stir well. Add celery, carrots, and cabbage, and bring to a boil over high heat. Reduce the heat to low, and simmer vegetables, covered, over low heat, for 10–12 minutes, or until vegetables are crisp-tender. Add fish and green beans, and cook an additional 3–5 minutes, or until fish is cooked through and flakes easily.

*Available in the Asian aisle of most supermarkets and in specialty markets.

3. Mix cornstarch with water, and stir cornstarch mixture into the pan. Cook for 1–2 minutes, or until slightly thickened. Season to taste with salt and red pepper flakes, and serve immediately.

Note: The dish can be prepared up to 1 day in advance and refrigerated, tightly covered. Reheat it over low heat, covered, until hot, stirring occasionally.

Variation:

- Substitute vegetable stock for the seafood stock, and substitute 1¼ pounds firm tofu, drained and cut into 1-inch cubes, for the fish.

While I really like Chinese chile paste with garlic, you can substitute either crushed red pepper flakes or hot red pepper sauce for it in any recipe.

Chapter 6:

Poultry Prowess: Soups and Stews with Chicken and Turkey

Chicken soup is now synonymous with comfort food. Why else would *Chicken Soup for the Soul* become such a popular book title?

There is evidence to support the idea that chicken stock really does contain medicinal qualities; perhaps your grandma was right all along. In 1993, University of Nebraska Medical Center researcher Dr. Stephen Rennard published a study stating that chicken soup contains a number of health-promoting substances, including an anti-inflammatory mechanism that eases the symptoms of upper respiratory tract infections. Other studies showed that the chicken soup was equally medicinal if made without vegetables; the source of the beneficial substances was the chicken itself.

There are two ways to create chicken soups—either from "scratch" or by using leftover chicken cooked another way. If you're doing the latter, then go ahead and use stock from your freezer, and cut up whatever chicken you have around. But if you're specifically cooking stock and chicken to make a soup, then look at the recipe that leads off this chapter; you get a rich stock with chicken meat that is tender but still has texture.

For chicken stews, I advocate using thighs, legs, and breasts, which are cut in half; they're bigger than the other pieces and they fit more neatly in the stew pot if cut. Save the wings separately for making baked or grilled wings for a picnic or snack; there's not enough meat on them to justify taking up room in the stew pot.

Rounding out the recipes in this chapter are a few dishes made with ground turkey; it's the meat I'm dubbing "the hamburger of the twenty-first century." It's less expensive than ground beef, contains less saturated fat, and cooks just as quickly.

CREATIVE CUTTING

Almost every permutation of chicken is now available in almost every supermarket—from whole birds of various sizes to delicate breast tenderloins. But it is far more economical to purchase a whole chicken and cut it up yourself than to buy one already cut. If it's a week when whole fryers (chickens between 3 pounds and 3½ pounds) are on sale, take advantage of it. I usually cut up between four and six chickens at a time; that yields enough various pieces for many meals.

Remember that *nothing goes to waste.* The giblets and any bones and skin should go into a bag for making Chicken Stock; the recipe is on page 23. Freeze the livers separately, and use them in another way; livers cannot be used for making stock. Then you can sort the remaining pieces by type and freeze them in separate bags. Here's a brief guide to becoming a poultry production line:

- **Cutting up whole chickens.** Start by pulling back the wings until the joints snap, then use the boning knife to cut through the ball joints and detach the wings. When holding the chicken on its side, you will see a natural curve outlining the boundary between the breast and the leg/thigh quarters. Use sharp kitchen shears to cut along this line. Cut the breast in half by scraping away the meat from the breastbone and using a small paring knife to remove the wishbone. Cut away the breastbone using the shears, and save it for stock. Divide the leg/thigh quarters by turning the pieces over and finding the joint joining them. Cut through the joint and sever the leg from the thigh.

- **Boning chicken breasts.** The price per pound for the edible meat is the lowest when you bone the breasts yourself, especially when they're sold as part of a whole chicken. Pull off the skin with your fingers, and then make an incision on either side of the breastbone, cutting down until you feel the bone resisting the knife. Working one side at a time, place the blade of your boning knife against the carcass, and scrape away the meat. You will then have two pieces: the large fillet and the small tenderloin. To trim the fillet, cut away any fat, and pound the meat gently between two sheets of plastic wrap to an even thickness. To trim the tenderloin, secure the tip of the tendon that will be visible with your free hand. Using a paring knife, scrape down the tendon, and the meat will push away.

Chicken Stock for Entree Soups

Most stock is made with scraps and trimmings, and after boiling it for many hours there's really nothing left to save. But cooking this recipe gives you a flavorful broth plus freshly cooked chicken in large pieces to cut up for the soup, and you'll have some left over, too. You can use it in future soups, or look at the many chicken salad recipes in other books in the *$3 Meals* series.

Yield: 3 quarts | **Active time:** 10 minutes | **Start to finish:** 3 hours

1 (3½–4-pound) chicken including giblets, liver reserved for another use
6 quarts water
2 celery ribs, rinsed and cut into thick slices
1 large onion, trimmed and quartered
2 carrots, trimmed, scrubbed, and cut into thick slices
1 tablespoon salt
2 tablespoons whole black peppercorns
4 garlic cloves, peeled
4 sprigs fresh parsley
1 teaspoon dried thyme
2 bay leaves

1. Rinse chicken inside and out. Place chicken and water in a large stockpot, and bring to a boil over high heat. Reduce the heat to low, and skim off foam that rises during the first 10–15 minutes of simmering. Simmer stock, uncovered, for 15 minutes, then add celery, onion, carrots, salt, peppercorns, garlic, parsley, thyme, and bay leaves. Simmer for an additional 1 hour.
2. Remove chicken from the stockpot with a slotted spoon, and set aside. When cool enough to handle, remove meat from bones, and discard bones and skin.
3. Raise the heat to medium, and cook vegetables and remaining stock for an additional 1 hour, or until liquid is reduced by ⅓.
4. Strain stock through a fine-meshed sieve, pushing with the back of a spoon to extract as much liquid as possible. Discard solids, spoon stock into smaller containers, and refrigerate. Remove and discard fat from surface of stock, then transfer stock to a variety of container sizes.

Note: The stock can be refrigerated and used within 3 days, or it can be frozen for up to 6 months.

Variation:

- For turkey stock, substitute ½ turkey breast or 1 leg and thigh quarter for the chicken, and cook the turkey for 1½ hours after adding the vegetables.

> The vegetables are added after the stock has simmered for a few minutes because it's easier to remove the scum that rises to the surface if there are no vegetables floating around.

Cheddar and Vegetable Chowder

This soup is a sure-fire kid pleaser, but the whole family will love it. The chicken and vegetables float in a creamy broth laced with heady cheddar cheese. Serve it with a tossed green salad and some crusty bread.

Yield: 4–6 servings | **Active time:** 15 minutes | **Start to finish:** 45 minutes

3 tablespoons unsalted butter
1 medium onion, peeled and diced
3 tablespoons all-purpose flour
2½ cups Chicken Stock (recipe on page 23) or purchased stock
1 large carrot, peeled and diced
2 celery ribs, rinsed, trimmed, and diced
½ pound redskin potatoes, scrubbed and cut into ¾-inch dice
2 tablespoons chopped fresh parsley
½ teaspoon dried thyme
2 cups half-and-half or whole milk
1 cup frozen peas, thawed
1½ cups grated sharp cheddar cheese
2–3 cups diced cooked chicken
Salt and freshly ground black pepper to taste

1. Melt butter in a 4-quart saucepan over medium-high heat. Add onion and cook, stirring frequently, for 3 minutes, or until onion is translucent. Add flour, and cook over low heat for 2 minutes, stirring constantly. Add stock gradually, and bring to a boil over medium-high heat.
2. Add carrot, celery, potatoes, parsley, and thyme to the pan. Bring to a boil, reduce the heat to low, and simmer soup, covered, for 12–15 minutes, or until vegetables are tender. Add half-and-half and peas to the pan, and bring back to a simmer.
3. Add cheese to soup by ½-cup measures, stirring until cheese melts before adding the next batch. Stir in chicken, season to taste with salt and pepper, and serve immediately.

Note: The soup can be prepared up to 2 days in advance and refrigerated, tightly covered. Reheat it over low heat, covered, until hot, stirring occasionally.

Variations:

- Substitute Swiss cheese for the cheddar cheese.
- Substitute cut green beans or lima beans for the peas.

It's always important to cook the flour as specified in a recipe to make any sort of white sauce or cream soup. Coating the proteins in the flour with fat keeps the sauce from tasting pasty.

Southwest Creamy Chicken, Corn, and Sweet Potato Chowder

Chipotle chiles are smoked jalapeño chiles that add a smoky nuance to this creamy chowder, which is flecked with corn and other vegetables. Some warm corn tortillas and a salad with avocado work well to complete the meal.

Yield: 4–6 servings | **Active time:** 20 minutes | **Start to finish:** 1 hour

1 pound boneless, skinless chicken thighs
3 tablespoons unsalted butter
1 green bell pepper, seeds and ribs removed, chopped
1 large onion, peeled and diced
2 garlic cloves, peeled and minced
2 large sweet potatoes, peeled and cut into ¾-inch dice
4 cups Chicken Stock (recipe on page 23) or purchased stock
2 canned chipotle chiles in adobo sauce, finely chopped
2 teaspoons adobo sauce
1 (15-ounce) can creamed corn
1 cup frozen corn, thawed
2 cups half-and-half or whole milk
Salt and freshly ground black pepper to taste
3 tablespoons chopped fresh cilantro

1. Rinse chicken and pat dry with paper towels. Cut chicken into ¾-inch dice.
2. Melt butter in a 4-quart saucepan over medium-high heat. Add chicken, and cook for 2 minutes, or until chicken is opaque. Add green bell pepper, onion, and garlic. Cook, stirring frequently, for 3 minutes, or until onion is translucent. Add sweet potatoes, stock, chipotle chiles, and adobo sauce to the saucepan, and stir well.
3. Bring to a boil over medium-high heat, then reduce the heat to low and simmer soup, covered, for 20–25 minutes. Add creamed corn, corn, and half-and-half, and simmer for 5 minutes, or until chicken is cooked through and no longer pink and vegetables are tender. Season to taste with salt and pepper, and serve immediately, sprinkling each serving with cilantro.

Note: The soup can be prepared up to 2 days in advance and refrigerated, tightly covered. Reheat it over low heat, covered, until hot, stirring occasionally.

Variation:

- Substitute 1 (4-ounce) can chopped mild green chiles, drained, for the chipotle chiles and adobo sauce for a less spicy soup.

> Cilantro is an herb used both in Hispanic and Asian cuisines, but I have discovered that people either love its musty flavor or think it tastes like soap. Flat-leaf Italian parsley can always be substituted if you don't like the flavor of cilantro.

Mexican Tortilla Soup

The flavor in this soup comes from a host of spices as well as two types of chiles. It also contains healthful beans and lots of vegetables, and it's garnished with crispy strips of tortilla! Flour tortillas or cornbread go nicely with it.

Yield: 4–6 servings | **Active time:** 20 minutes | **Start to finish:** 45 minutes

SOUP

1 pound boneless, skinless chicken thighs
2 tablespoons olive oil
1 medium onion, peeled and diced
1 poblano chile, seeds and ribs removed, chopped
3 garlic cloves, peeled and minced
1–2 jalapeño or serrano chiles, seeds and ribs removed, finely chopped
2 teaspoons ground cumin
1½ teaspoons dried oregano
1 teaspoon ground coriander
6 cups Chicken Stock (recipe on page 23) or purchased stock
2 tablespoons tomato paste
1 (15-ounce) can red kidney beans, drained and rinsed (optional)
1 large carrot, peeled and sliced
2 celery ribs, rinsed, trimmed, and sliced
Salt and freshly ground black pepper to taste

GARNISH

Vegetable oil spray
3–4 (6-inch) corn tortillas
½ cup grated Monterey Jack cheese
¼ cup chopped fresh cilantro
4–6 lime wedges

1. Rinse chicken and pat dry with paper towels. Cut chicken into ¾-inch dice.

2. Heat oil in a 4-quart saucepan over medium-high heat. Add chicken, and cook for 2 minutes, or until chicken is opaque. Add onion, poblano chile, garlic, and jalapeño chile. Cook, stirring frequently, for 3 minutes, or until onion is translucent. Add cumin, oregano, and coriander, and cook for 1 minute, stirring constantly.
3. Add stock and tomato paste, and stir well to dissolve tomato paste. Add kidney beans (if using), carrot, and celery, and bring to a boil over high heat, stirring occasionally. Reduce the heat to low, and simmer soup, partially covered, for 15 minutes, or until chicken is cooked through and no longer pink and vegetables are tender. Season to taste with salt and pepper.
4. While soup simmers, prepare tortilla strips. Preheat the oven to 375°F, line a baking sheet with heavy-duty aluminum foil, and grease foil with vegetable oil spray. Cut tortillas into ½-inch-wide strips, and arrange strips on the prepared baking sheet. Spray tops of strips with vegetable oil spray. Bake strips for 5–7 minutes, or until crisp. Remove the pan from the oven, and set aside.
5. To serve, ladle soup into bowls, and garnish each serving with tortilla strips, cheese, cilantro, and lime. Serve immediately.

Note: The soup can be prepared up to 2 days in advance and refrigerated, tightly covered. Reheat it over low heat, covered, until hot, stirring occasionally.

The tortilla strips can be made up to 2 days in advance and kept at room temperature. Do not prepare the other garnishes until just prior to serving.

Variation:

- Omit the jalapeño chile and substitute a small green bell pepper for the poblano chile for a mild dish.

Poblanos are the mildest of the chiles in the pantheon of hot peppers. They're about 4 inches long, tapered, and very dark green and shiny. Anaheim peppers are the best ones to substitute.

Sweet and Sour Cabbage Soup

In my opinion, healthful cabbage is a much maligned and under-utilized vegetable, and it's always one of the most reasonably priced in the produce department. It becomes silky and smooth in this hearty soup, with a slight nuance of sweet and sour in the broth. Serve it with some crusty peasant bread, like pumpernickel, and a tossed salad.

Yield: 4–6 servings | **Active time:** 20 minutes | **Start to finish:** 1½ hours

1 tablespoon vegetable oil
¾ pound ground turkey
2 medium onions, peeled and chopped
2 garlic cloves, peeled and minced
1½ pounds (about ½ head) green cabbage, shredded
1 (28-ounce) can diced tomatoes, undrained
6 cups Chicken Stock (recipe on page 23) or purchased stock
1 Granny Smith apple, peeled, cored, and grated
⅔ cup chopped raisins
3 tablespoons cider vinegar
3 tablespoons firmly packed dark brown sugar
1 teaspoon dry mustard powder
½ teaspoon ground ginger
Salt and freshly ground black pepper to taste

1. Heat oil in a 4-quart saucepan over medium-high heat. Add turkey, breaking up lumps with a fork, and cook for 2 minutes. Add onions and garlic, and cook, stirring frequently, for 3 minutes, or until onion is translucent.
2. Add cabbage, tomatoes, and stock, and bring to a boil. Reduce the heat to low, cover the pan, and simmer for 30 minutes.
3. Stir in apple, raisins, vinegar, brown sugar, mustard, and ginger. Simmer soup, uncovered, for 30 minutes, or until cabbage is very soft. Season to taste with salt and pepper, and serve immediately.

Note: The soup can be prepared up to 2 days in advance and refrigerated, tightly covered. Reheat it over low heat, covered, until hot, stirring occasionally.

Variations:

- Substitute red cabbage for the green cabbage.
- Replace the raisins with dried currants or chopped dried apricots.
- Substitute ground beef for the turkey, and substitute beef stock for the chicken stock.

> Cabbage belongs to the same family of vegetables as cauliflower and Brussels sprouts. All are a great source of vitamin C. Cabbage also contains indoles, which current research indicates may lower the risk of various forms of cancer.

Italian Chicken, Bean, and Barley Soup

Barley is an ancient grain, and it creates a thick and robust chicken soup flavored with many vegetables and herbs as well as delicate cannellini beans. Serve it with garlic bread and a tossed salad to complete the meal.

Yield: 4–6 servings | **Active time:** 20 minutes | **Start to finish:** 1 hour

1 pound boneless, skinless chicken thighs
3 tablespoons olive oil
1 large onion, peeled and diced
3 garlic cloves, peeled and minced
2 celery ribs, rinsed, trimmed, and sliced
2 carrots, peeled and sliced
1 green bell pepper, seeds and ribs removed, diced
3/4 cup pearl barley, rinsed well
5 cups Chicken Stock (recipe on page 23) or purchased stock
1 (15-ounce) can cannellini beans, drained and rinsed
1 (14.5-ounce) can diced tomatoes, undrained
1 (8-ounce) can tomato sauce
2 tablespoons chopped fresh parsley
2 teaspoons Italian seasoning
1 bay leaf
1 (10-ounce) package frozen leaf spinach, thawed and drained
2/3 cup freshly grated Parmesan cheese
Salt and freshly ground black pepper to taste

1. Rinse chicken and pat dry with paper towels. Cut chicken into 3/4-inch dice.
2. Heat oil in a 4-quart saucepan over medium-high heat. Add chicken, and cook for 2 minutes, or until chicken is opaque. Add onion, garlic, celery, carrot, and green bell pepper, and cook, stirring frequently, for 3 minutes, or until onion is translucent.
3. Add barley, stock, beans, tomatoes, tomato sauce, parsley, Italian seasoning, and bay leaf. Stir well. Bring to a boil, then reduce the heat to low and simmer soup, covered, for 35–40 minutes, or until chicken is cooked through and no longer pink and vegetables are tender.

4. Stir in spinach and Parmesan cheese, and cook for 5 minutes. Remove and discard bay leaf, season to taste with salt and pepper, and ladle soup into bowls.

Note: The soup can be prepared up to 2 days in advance and refrigerated, tightly covered. Reheat it over low heat, covered, until hot, stirring occasionally.

Variation:

- Substitute 1 bunch fresh Swiss chard, rinsed and shredded, for the spinach.

> You can substitute cooked chicken for the raw chicken specified in this or any of these soup recipes. Add it at the end of the cooking time; in this case it would be added with the spinach.

Thai Chicken Noodle Soup

Fiery chile, creamy coconut milk, and aromatic ginger flavor this Asian soup that is sold all around Thailand. I've used egg noodles rather than rice noodles. Try some cucumbers marinated in rice vinegar as a salad.

Yield: 4–6 servings | **Active time:** 20 minutes | **Start to finish:** 40 minutes

- 6 ounces medium egg noodles
- 2 tablespoons vegetable oil
- 6 scallions, white parts and 4 inches of green tops, rinsed, trimmed, and cut into 3/4-inch lengths
- 3 garlic cloves, peeled and minced
- 1 Thai, jalapeño, or serrano chile, seeds and ribs removed, finely chopped
- 1 tablespoon grated fresh ginger
- 2 teaspoons grated lemon zest
- 6 cups Chicken Stock (recipe on page 23) or purchased stock
- 1 cup light coconut milk
- 3 tablespoons fish sauce (*nam pla*)*
- 2 tablespoons lemon juice
- 3–4 cups diced cooked chicken
- 3 ripe plum tomatoes, rinsed, cored, seeded, and diced
- Salt and freshly ground black pepper to taste
- 2 tablespoons chopped fresh cilantro

1. Bring a large pot of salted water to a boil over high heat. Add egg noodles, and cook according to package directions until al dente. Drain, and set aside.
2. While the noodles cook, heat oil in a 4-quart saucepan over medium-high heat. Add scallions, garlic, chile, ginger, and lemon zest, and cook, stirring frequently, for 3 minutes, or until scallions are translucent.
3. Add stock, coconut milk, fish sauce, and lemon juice, and bring to a boil over medium-high heat, stirring occasionally. Add chicken and tomatoes, and cook for an additional 3 minutes. Stir in noodles, season to taste with salt and pepper, and serve immediately, sprinkling each serving with cilantro.

*Available in the Asian aisle of most supermarkets and in specialty markets.

Note: The soup can be prepared up to 2 days in advance and refrigerated, tightly covered. Refrigerate the noodles separately. Reheat it over low heat, covered, until hot, stirring occasionally.

Variations:

- Substitute rice or small pasta for the egg noodles.
- Add 2 cups shredded fresh spinach or bok choy leaves along with the chicken.

If you're cooking a soup that contains pasta or egg noodles and plan to refrigerate it before serving it, don't add the pasta when you cook it. The pasta can absorb more liquid during storage and become "soggy."

Southern Chicken and Vegetable Stew with Cornmeal Dumplings

Creole seasoning and some healthful vegetables are simmered and then topped with flavorful dumplings that are like light pillows once they puff and cook. A tossed salad is all you need to complete the meal.

Yield: 4–6 servings | **Active time:** 20 minutes | **Start to finish:** 1 hour

STEW

1¼ pounds boneless, skinless chicken thighs
Salt and freshly ground black pepper to taste
3 tablespoons vegetable oil
1 large onion, peeled and diced
3 garlic cloves, peeled and minced
2 celery ribs, rinsed, trimmed, and sliced
1 small green bell pepper, seeds and ribs removed, diced
2 tablespoons Creole seasoning
1 teaspoon dried thyme
1 teaspoon dried oregano
2 bay leaves
2 (14.5-ounce) cans diced tomatoes, undrained
2 cups Chicken Stock (recipe on page 23) or purchased stock
3 tablespoons chopped fresh parsley
1 (10-ounce) package frozen black-eyed peas, thawed
1 cup fresh corn kernels or frozen corn kernels, thawed

DUMPLINGS

½ cup all-purpose flour
⅓ cup cornmeal
2 tablespoons chopped fresh parsley
1 teaspoon baking powder
¼ teaspoon salt
1 large egg
2 tablespoons whole milk
2 tablespoons unsalted butter, melted

1. Rinse chicken and pat dry with paper towels. Cut chicken into 1½-inch cubes, and sprinkle cubes with salt and pepper.
2. Heat oil in a deep skillet over medium-high heat. Add chicken, and cook for 2 minutes, or until chicken is opaque. Add onion, garlic, celery, and green bell pepper, and cook, stirring frequently, for 3 minutes, or until onion is translucent. Reduce the heat to low, and add Creole seasoning, thyme, oregano, and bay leaves. Cook for 1 minute, stirring constantly.
3. Add tomatoes, stock, and parsley, and stir well. Bring to a boil and cook over medium heat, covered, stirring occasionally, for 25–30 minutes, or until chicken is cooked through and no longer pink.
4. While stew cooks, prepare dumpling batter. In a medium bowl, stir together flour, cornmeal, parsley, baking powder, and salt. In a small bowl, whisk together egg, milk, and melted butter. Add liquids to flour mixture, and stir with a fork just until combined.
5. Add black-eyed peas and corn to stew. Remove and discard bay leaves, and season to taste with salt and pepper.
6. Drop dumpling batter into 8–12 mounds on top of stew. Cover and cook for an additional 12–15 minutes, or until dumplings are puffed and cooked through. Do not lift the lid while dumplings steam. Serve immediately.

Note: The stew can be prepared up to 2 days in advance and refrigerated, tightly covered. Reheat it over low heat, covered, until it reaches a simmer, stirring occasionally. Then prepare dumpling batter and cook as directed.

Variation:

- Substitute vegetable stock for the chicken stock, and substitute 1 pound acorn or butternut squash, peeled and cut into ¾-inch cubes, for the chicken.

Chicken Stew with Dried Fruit

A combination of sweet and succulent dried fruits balanced by herbs and sharp Dijon mustard flavor this family-pleasing chicken stew. Serve it with a steamed green vegetable on top of rice.

Yield: 4–6 servings | **Active time:** 20 minutes | **Start to finish:** 1¼ hours

- 1 (3½–4-pound) frying chicken, cut into serving pieces, each breast half cut crosswise in half
- 1 lemon
- 1 tablespoon unsalted butter
- 1 tablespoon vegetable oil
- 1 large onion, peeled and diced
- 1 carrot, peeled and sliced
- 2 garlic cloves, peeled and minced
- ½ cup dry white wine
- 2 cups Chicken Stock (recipe on page 23) or purchased stock
- ½ cup diced pitted prunes
- ½ cup dried cranberries
- ½ cup diced dried apricots
- ¼ cup Dijon mustard
- 2 tablespoons chopped fresh parsley
- ½ teaspoon dried thyme
- Salt and freshly ground black pepper to taste
- 3 cups cooked brown or white rice, hot

1. Preheat the oven broiler, and line a broiler pan with heavy-duty aluminum foil. Rinse chicken and pat dry with paper towels. Broil chicken pieces for 3–5 minutes per side, or until browned. Set chicken aside, and preheat the oven to 375°F. Grate zest from lemon, and squeeze juice from lemon. Set aside.
2. Heat butter and oil in a Dutch oven over medium-high heat. Add onion, carrot, and garlic, and cook, stirring frequently, for 3 minutes, or until onion is translucent. Add wine, and cook for 3 minutes. Add lemon zest, lemon juice, stock, prunes, cranberries, apricots, mustard, parsley, and thyme, and stir well. Add chicken, and bring to a boil on top of the stove. Cover the Dutch oven, and bake chicken for 1–1¼ hours, or until chicken is cooked through and no longer pink.

3. Remove 1 cup solids from the Dutch oven with a slotted spoon, and transfer to a food processor fitted with the steel blade or to a blender. Be careful not to fill the beaker too full when blending hot ingredients. Puree until smooth, and stir puree back into juices in the pan. Season to taste with salt and pepper, and serve immediately.

Note: The dish can be prepared up to 2 days in advance and refrigerated, tightly covered. Reheat it, covered, in a 350°F oven for 20–25 minutes, or until hot.

Variation:

- Substitute 1¼ pounds boneless pork loin, cut into 1-inch cubes, for the chicken.

There are many ways to thicken stews, and this recipe uses one of them—pureeing some of the ingredients. This not only thickens the broth, but it also flavors it.

Chicken Marseilles

This dish hailing from the sunny region of Southern France is similar to the city's famed bouillabaisse, but made with chicken. The broth remains thin, and it's absorbed by a slice of thick toast. A garlicky sauce, similar to French aioli, tops the dish.

Yield: 4–6 servings | **Active time:** 25 minutes | **Start to finish:** 1½ hours

CHICKEN

1 (3½–4-pound) frying chicken, cut into serving pieces, each breast half cut crosswise in half
1 orange
3 tablespoons olive oil
1 large onion, peeled and diced
3 garlic cloves, peeled and minced
¾ cup dry white wine
2 cups Chicken Stock (recipe on page 23) or purchased stock
1 (14.5-ounce) can diced tomatoes, undrained
1 carrot, peeled and diced
2 celery ribs, rinsed, trimmed, and diced
3 tablespoons chopped fresh parsley
1 teaspoon dried thyme
1 bay leaf
Salt and freshly ground black pepper to taste
Vegetable oil spray
12 (¾-inch-thick) slices French or Italian bread
½ cup freshly grated Parmesan cheese

SAUCE

½ cup mayonnaise
2 garlic cloves, peeled and minced
1 tablespoon lemon juice
Salt and freshly ground black pepper to taste

1. For chicken, preheat the oven broiler, and line a broiler pan with heavy-duty aluminum foil. Rinse chicken and pat dry with paper towels. Broil chicken pieces for 3–5 minutes per side, or until browned. Set chicken aside, and preheat the oven to 375°F. Grate zest from orange, and squeeze juice from fruit.
2. Heat oil in a Dutch oven over medium-high heat. Add onion and garlic, and cook, stirring frequently, for 3 minutes, or until onion is translucent. Add wine, raise the heat to high, and cook for 3 minutes.
3. Add chicken, orange zest, orange juice, stock, tomatoes, carrot, celery, parsley, thyme, and bay leaf to the Dutch oven. Bring to a boil on top of the stove. Cover the Dutch oven, and bake chicken for 1–1¼ hours, or until chicken is cooked through and no longer pink. Remove and discard bay leaf, and season to taste with salt and pepper.
4. While chicken bakes, cover a baking sheet with aluminum foil, and spray foil with vegetable oil spray. Arrange bread slices on the baking sheet, and sprinkle bread with Parmesan cheese. Bake for 15–18 minutes, or until toasts brown. Remove from the oven, and set aside.
5. For sauce, combine mayonnaise, garlic, lemon juice, salt, and pepper in a small bowl. Stir well, and refrigerate until ready to serve.
6. To serve, place toast slices in the bottoms of shallow bowls, and arrange chicken on top. Ladle broth over chicken, and serve immediately, passing sauce separately.

Note: The dish can be prepared up to 2 days in advance and refrigerated, tightly covered. Reheat it, covered, in a 350°F oven for 20–25 minutes, or until hot. The sauce and toast can be prepared at the same time; refrigerate sauce and keep toasts at room temperature in an airtight container.

Variation:

- Substitute red wine for the white wine, omit the orange juice and zest, and substitute 2 teaspoons Italian seasoning for the thyme.

Belgian Chicken Stew

This recipe is similar in concept to *Carbonnades à la Flamande,* a Belgian beef stew made with caramelized onions and beer. Serve it on buttered egg noodles, with a tossed salad on the side.

Yield: 4–6 servings | **Active time:** 30 minutes | **Start to finish:** 1¾ hours

1 (3½–4-pound) frying chicken, cut into serving pieces, each breast half cut crosswise in half
3 tablespoons unsalted butter
2 tablespoons olive oil
2 large onions, peeled, halved lengthwise, and thinly sliced
2 garlic cloves, peeled and minced
1 teaspoon granulated sugar
Salt and freshly ground black pepper to taste
1 (12-ounce) bottle or can beer
¾ cup Chicken Stock (recipe on page 23) or purchased stock
3 tablespoons chopped fresh parsley
2 tablespoons firmly packed dark brown sugar
2 teaspoons Dijon mustard
½ teaspoon dried thyme
1 bay leaf
1 tablespoon cornstarch
2 tablespoons cold water
3 cups cooked egg noodles, buttered

1. Preheat the oven broiler, and line a broiler pan with heavy-duty aluminum foil. Rinse chicken and pat dry with paper towels. Broil chicken pieces for 3–5 minutes per side, or until browned. Set chicken aside, and preheat the oven to 375°F.
2. While chicken browns, heat butter and oil in a Dutch oven over medium heat. Add onions and garlic, toss to coat with fat, and cook, covered, for 10 minutes. Uncover the pan, raise the heat to medium-high, and sprinkle onions with sugar, salt, and pepper. Cook, stirring occasionally, for 10–12 minutes, or until onions are lightly browned.
3. Add chicken, beer, stock, parsley, brown sugar, mustard, thyme, and bay leaf to the Dutch oven. Bring to a boil on top of the stove. Cover the Dutch oven, and bake chicken for 1–1¼ hours, or until chicken is cooked through and no longer pink.

4. Mix cornstarch and cold water in a small cup. Add cornstarch mixture, and cook on top of the stove over medium heat for 2 minutes, or until slightly thickened. Remove and discard bay leaf, season to taste with salt and pepper, and serve immediately with noodles.

Note: The stew can be prepared up to 2 days in advance and refrigerated, tightly covered. Reheat it, covered, in a 350°F oven for 20–25 minutes, or until hot.

Variation:

- Substitute 1¼ pounds boneless pork loin, cut into 1-inch cubes, for the chicken.

> When you're browning onions, what you are doing is caramelizing the natural sugars in the vegetable. It may come as quite a shock to you to learn that an onion, which is so harsh when raw, really does contain a lot of natural sugar. Sprinkling the onions with sugar and salt speeds up the browning process.

Moroccan Chicken Stew

Garbanzo beans have the nuttiest flavor and meatiest texture of the legumes, and they are used extensively in Mediterranean cuisines. They are joined in this chicken dish by colorful green beans and a number of spices. Serve this dish with couscous to enjoy the sauce.

Yield: 4–6 servings | **Active time:** 20 minutes | **Start to finish:** 1¼ hours

1 (3½–4-pound) frying chicken, cut into serving pieces, each breast half cut crosswise in half
2 tablespoons olive oil
1 large onion, peeled and diced
3 garlic cloves, peeled and minced
2 carrots, peeled and sliced
3 tablespoons paprika
2 tablespoons ground cumin
1 tablespoon ground coriander
2½ cups Chicken Stock (recipe on page 23) or purchased stock
¼ cup balsamic vinegar
1 (15-ounce) can garbanzo beans, drained and rinsed
1 (10-ounce) package frozen cut green beans, thawed
Salt and freshly ground black pepper to taste

1. Preheat the oven broiler, and line a broiler pan with heavy-duty aluminum foil. Rinse chicken and pat dry with paper towels. Broil chicken pieces for 3–5 minutes per side, or until browned. Set chicken aside, and preheat the oven to 375°F.
2. Heat oil in a Dutch oven over medium-high heat. Add onion, garlic, and carrots, and cook, stirring frequently, for 3 minutes, or until onion is translucent. Add paprika, cumin, and coriander, and cook for 1 minute, stirring constantly. Add stock, vinegar, and garbanzo beans, and stir well. Add chicken, and bring to a boil on top of the stove. Cover the Dutch oven, and bake chicken for 45 minutes.
3. Add green beans, and cook for an additional 15–20 minutes, or until chicken is cooked through and no longer pink. Season to taste with salt and pepper, and serve immediately.

Note: The dish can be prepared up to 2 days in advance and refrigerated, tightly covered. Reheat it, covered, in a 350°F oven for 20–25 minutes, or until hot.

Variation:

- Substitute 1¼ pounds boneless pork loin, cut into 1-inch cubes, for the chicken.

> While canned beans are only minimally processed, part of that processing includes the addition of salt, so they are high in sodium. If you are following a low-sodium diet, always cook beans from dried beans yourself. One can of beans is equivalent to 1½ cups of cooked beans.

Caribbean Chicken Stew with Plantains

This spicy stew is based on a dish traditional to the Dominican Republic. Serve it with a tossed salad over rice.

Yield: 4–6 servings | **Active time:** 25 minutes | **Start to finish:** 1 hour

- 1¼ pounds boneless, skinless chicken thighs
- 2 green plantains
- ¼ cup olive oil
- 1 large onion, peeled and diced
- 1 green bell pepper, seeds and ribs removed, diced
- 3 garlic cloves, peeled and minced
- 1 jalapeño or serrano chile, seeds and ribs removed, finely chopped
- 1 tablespoon dried oregano
- ½ teaspoon ground allspice
- 2 cups Chicken Stock (recipe on page 23) or purchased stock
- 1 (14.5-ounce) can diced tomatoes, undrained
- 2 tablespoons cider vinegar
- ¼ cup chopped fresh cilantro, divided
- 1 pound redskin potatoes, scrubbed and cut into 1-inch cubes
- 1 (10-ounce) package frozen corn, thawed
- 3 cups cooked brown or white rice, hot

1. Rinse chicken and pat dry with paper towels. Cut chicken into 1½-inch cubes. Set aside. Trim both ends from plantain, and cut 4 slits into the peel lengthwise, being careful not to cut into the flesh. Microwave plantains on Medium (50 percent power) for 1 minute. Pull off the peel, using a paring knife if necessary. Cut plantains into 1½-inch chunks, and set aside.
2. Heat oil in a deep skillet or saucepan over medium-high heat. Add chicken, and cook for 2 minutes, or until chicken is opaque. Remove chicken from the pan with a slotted spoon, and set aside. Add onion, green bell pepper, garlic, and chile to the pan, and cook, stirring frequently, for 3 minutes, or until onion is translucent. Add oregano and allspice, and cook for 1 minute, stirring constantly.

3. Return chicken to the pan, and add stock, tomatoes, vinegar, and 2 tablespoons cilantro. Bring to a boil over medium-high heat, stirring occasionally. Reduce the heat to low, cover the pan, and cook for 10 minutes. Add plantains and potatoes, and cook for an additional 30 minutes, or until chicken is cooked through and no longer pink and vegetables are tender. Add corn, and simmer 3 minutes. Season to taste with salt and pepper, and serve immediately, sprinkling each serving with remaining cilantro.

Note: The dish can be prepared up to 2 days in advance and refrigerated, tightly covered. Reheat it, covered, in a 350°F oven for 20–25 minutes, or until hot.

Variation:

- Substitute vegetable stock for the chicken stock, and substitute 1½ pounds zucchini or yellow squash, cut into 1½-inch cubes, for the chicken.

Proper storage can give extra life to leafy herbs like cilantro, parsley, and dill. Treat them like a bouquet of flowers; trim the stems when you get home from the market and then stand the bunch in a glass of water in the refrigerator.

Spicy Mexican Chicken Stew

Potatoes and carrots join the chicken in this stew made spicy with smoky chipotle chiles in a tomato sauce. Serve the dish with warmed flour tortillas or cornbread, and a bowl of guacamole.

Yield: 4–6 servings | **Active time:** 20 minutes | **Start to finish:** 40 minutes

1¼ pounds boneless, skinless chicken thighs
Salt and freshly ground black pepper to taste
3 tablespoons olive oil, divided
1 small onion, peeled and diced
3 garlic cloves, peeled and minced
1 (14.5-ounce) can diced tomatoes, undrained
2 chipotle chiles in adobo sauce
1 teaspoon dried oregano
2 cups Chicken Stock (recipe on page 23) or purchased stock
1 pound redskin potatoes, scrubbed and cut into 1-inch cubes
1 large carrot, peeled and sliced
¾–1 cup grated Monterey Jack cheese

1. Rinse chicken and pat dry with paper towels. Cut chicken into 1-inch cubes, sprinkle with salt and pepper, and set aside.
2. Heat 1 tablespoon oil in a large skillet over medium-high heat. Add onion and garlic, and cook, stirring frequently, for 3 minutes, or until onion is translucent. Transfer mixture to a food processor fitted with the steel blade or to a blender. Be careful not to fill the beaker too full when blending hot ingredients. Add tomatoes, chiles, and oregano, and puree until smooth.
3. Heat remaining 2 tablespoons oil in the skillet over medium-high heat. Add puree, lower the heat to medium, and cook sauce for 5 minutes.
4. Add stock, chicken, potatoes, and carrot to the skillet. Bring to a boil over medium-high heat, stirring occasionally. Cover the skillet, and cook for 12–15 minutes, or until chicken is cooked through and no longer pink and vegetables are tender. Season to taste with salt and pepper, and serve immediately, sprinkling each serving with cheese.

Note: The dish can be prepared up to 2 days in advance and refrigerated, tightly covered. Reheat it, covered, in a 350°F oven for 20–25 minutes, or until hot.

Variations:

- Substitute sweet potatoes for the redskin potatoes.
- Substitute 1 (4-ounce) can diced mild green chiles, drained, for the chipotle chiles, for a milder dish.

The method of cooking a sauce *after* the ingredients have been pureed (rather than before they are pureed) is common in Mexican cooking. The sauce is also made far more quickly than if the ingredients are cooked first.

Chinese Red-Cooked Chicken Stew

Stews in traditional Chinese cooking are called "sandpots" for the earthenware vessel in which they were cooked. There is a tremendous amount of flavor in this moderately spicy dish. Serve it over rice.

Yield: 4–6 servings | **Active time:** 25 minutes | **Start to finish:** 1½ hours

- 1 (3½–4-pound) frying chicken, cut into serving pieces, with each breast half cut crosswise in half
- 1 orange
- 2½ cups water
- ½ cup soy sauce
- ½ cup dry sherry
- ¼ cup firmly packed light brown sugar
- 4 scallions, white parts and 4 inches of green tops, trimmed, rinsed, and sliced, white parts and green tops kept separate
- 3 tablespoons grated fresh ginger
- 2 garlic cloves, peeled and minced
- ½ cup chopped fresh cilantro, divided
- ½ teaspoon Chinese five-spice powder*
- ½ teaspoon crushed red pepper flakes
- 2 carrots, peeled and sliced on the diagonal
- 3 cups sliced bok choy
- 1 (10-ounce) package frozen sliced green beans, thawed
- 1 tablespoon cornstarch
- 2 tablespoons cold water
- Salt and freshly ground black pepper to taste
- 3 cups cooked brown or white rice, hot

1. Preheat the oven broiler, and line a broiler pan with heavy-duty aluminum foil. Rinse chicken and pat dry with paper towels. Broil chicken pieces for 3–5 minutes per side, or until browned. Set chicken aside, and preheat the oven to 375°F. Grate zest from orange and squeeze juice from fruit, straining out seeds, if necessary. Set aside.
2. Combine orange zest, orange juice, water, soy sauce, sherry, brown sugar, white parts of scallions, ginger, garlic, ¼ cup cilantro, Chinese five-spice powder, and red pepper flakes in a Dutch oven. Bring to a boil over high heat, stirring occasionally. Reduce the heat to low, and simmer sauce, uncovered, for 10 minutes.

*Available in the Asian aisle of most supermarkets and in specialty markets.

3. Add chicken and carrot to the Dutch oven, and bring to a boil on top of the stove. Cover the Dutch oven, transfer it to the oven, and bake chicken for 30 minutes. Add bok choy and green beans to the Dutch oven, and bake for an additional 30–40 minutes, or until chicken is cooked through and no longer pink.
4. Mix cornstarch and cold water in a small cup. Add cornstarch mixture, and cook on top of the stove over medium heat for 1–2 minutes, or until slightly thickened. Season to taste with salt and pepper, and serve immediately, sprinkling each serving with remaining cilantro and sliced green scallion tops.

Note: The dish can be prepared up to 2 days in advance and refrigerated, tightly covered. Reheat it, covered, in a 350°F oven for 20–25 minutes, or until hot.

Variation:

- Substitute 1¼ pounds boneless pork loin, cut into 1-inch cubes, for the chicken.

The zest of citrus fruit is only the very thin colored surface; it is there that the aromatic oils are located. The white pith beneath that colored surface is very bitter and should not be grated.

Chinese Chicken Curry

While we associate curry with Indian food, the spice is also used in the Caribbean and has a role in Chinese-American food. The vegetables in this dish remain crisp, and the sauce should be enjoyed with rice.

Yield: 4–6 servings | **Active time:** 20 minutes | **Start to finish:** 1¼ hours

1 (3½–4-pound) frying chicken, cut into serving pieces, each breast half cut crosswise in half
3 tablespoons Asian sesame oil*
4 scallions, white parts and 4 inches of green tops, rinsed, trimmed, and chopped
4 garlic cloves, peeled and minced
2 tablespoons grated fresh ginger
1 jalapeño or serrano chile, seeds and ribs removed, finely chopped
2 tablespoons curry powder
½ teaspoon Chinese five-spice powder*
1½ cups Chicken Stock (recipe on page 23) or purchased stock
1 cup light coconut milk
2 tablespoons rice vinegar
2 tablespoons firmly packed dark brown sugar
2 tablespoons soy sauce
2 tablespoons vegetable oil
1 large onion, peeled, halved, and cut into ½-inch slices
1 carrot, peeled and cut into ½-inch slices on the diagonal
1 green bell pepper, seeds and ribs removed, cut into ½-inch slices
2 celery ribs, rinsed, trimmed, and cut into ½-inch slices on the diagonal
1 tablespoon cornstarch
2 tablespoons cold water
Salt and freshly ground black pepper to taste
3 cups cooked brown or white rice, hot

1. Preheat the oven broiler, and line a broiler pan with heavy-duty aluminum foil. Rinse chicken and pat dry with paper towels. Broil chicken pieces for 3–5 minutes per side, or until browned. Set chicken aside, and preheat the oven to 375°F.

*Available in the Asian aisle of most supermarkets and in specialty markets.

2. While chicken browns, heat sesame oil in a Dutch oven over medium-high heat. Add scallions, garlic, ginger, and chile, and cook, stirring frequently, for 3 minutes, or until scallions are translucent. Add curry powder and five-spice powder, and cook for 1 minute, stirring constantly.
3. Add stock, coconut milk, vinegar, brown sugar, and soy sauce, and stir well. Add chicken, and bring to a boil on top of the stove. Cover the Dutch oven, transfer it to the oven, and bake chicken for 30 minutes.
4. While chicken cooks, heat vegetable oil in a large skillet over medium-high heat. Add onion, carrot, bell pepper, and celery. Cook, stirring frequently, for 3 minutes, or until onion is translucent.
5. Add vegetables to the Dutch oven, and cook for 15–20 minutes, or until vegetables are crisp-tender and chicken is cooked through and no longer pink.
6. Mix cornstarch and cold water in a small cup. Add cornstarch mixture to the stew, and cook on top of the stove over medium heat for 1–2 minutes, or until slightly thickened. Season to taste with salt and pepper, and serve immediately.

Note: The chicken can be prepared up to 2 days in advance and refrigerated, tightly covered. Reheat it, covered, in a 350°F oven for 20–25 minutes, or until hot.

Variation:

- Substitute 1¼ pounds boneless country pork ribs or pork loin, cut into 1-inch cubes, for the chicken.

Turkey Chili Blanca

Blanca means "white" in Spanish, and that's the color of this tomato-free thick and flavorful stew made with ground turkey and white beans, thickened with barley. Serve it with some cornbread and a tossed salad.

Yield: 4–6 servings | **Active time:** 20 minutes | **Start to finish:** 55 minutes

- 2 tablespoons olive oil
- 1 medium onion, peeled and diced
- 4 garlic cloves, peeled and minced
- ½ green bell pepper, seeds and ribs removed, chopped
- 1 large jalapeño or serrano chile, seeds and ribs removed, finely chopped
- 1 pound ground turkey
- 1½ tablespoons ground cumin
- 1½ teaspoons dried oregano
- 4 cups Chicken Stock (recipe on page 23) or purchased stock
- ⅓ cup pearl barley
- 2 (15-ounce) cans cannellini beans, drained and rinsed
- ¼ cup chopped fresh cilantro
- Salt and hot red pepper sauce to taste
- 4 scallions, white parts and 3 inches of green tops, rinsed, trimmed, and sliced
- ½ cup grated Monterey Jack cheese
- ½ cup sour cream

1. Heat oil in a large saucepan over medium-high heat. Add onion, garlic, green bell pepper, and chile. Cook, stirring frequently, for 3 minutes, or until onion is translucent. Add turkey, breaking up lumps with a fork, and cook for 3 minutes. Add cumin and oregano, and cook for 1 minute, stirring constantly.
2. Add stock and barley, and bring to a boil over medium-high heat. Reduce the heat to low, cover the pan, and simmer chili for 30 minutes, stirring occasionally.
3. Add beans and cilantro, and simmer chili, uncovered, stirring occasionally, for 15–25 minutes, or until barley is tender. Season to taste with salt and hot red pepper sauce. Serve immediately, passing scallions, cheese, and sour cream separately.

Note: The dish can be prepared up to 2 days in advance and refrigerated, tightly covered. Reheat it, covered, over low heat, stirring occasionally, until hot.

Variation:

- Substitute ground beef for the ground turkey, and substitute beef stock for the chicken stock.

When judging the heat of chile peppers, a good rule to follow is that the smaller the pepper, the hotter the pepper. That's why the same number of large jalapeño chiles and much smaller serrano chiles is listed.

Asian Turkey Chili

This is as hearty a bean dish as you could find in any cuisine; the black beans are flavored with a wide range of Asian flavors. Serve it over aromatic jasmine rice to form a complete protein, with some crunchy crudités on the side.

Yield: 4–6 servings | **Active time:** 15 minutes | **Start to finish:** 2 hours, including 1 hour to soak beans

1½ cups dried black beans
2 tablespoons Asian sesame oil*
8 scallions, white parts and 3 inches of green tops, rinsed, trimmed, and sliced
3 garlic cloves, peeled and minced
2 tablespoons grated fresh ginger
1 pound ground turkey
4 cups Chicken Stock (recipe on page 23) or purchased stock
½ cup dry sherry
¼ cup hoisin sauce*
¼ cup soy sauce
3 tablespoons rice vinegar
2 tablespoons Chinese black bean sauce*
2 teaspoons Chinese chile paste with garlic*
2 teaspoons granulated sugar
Salt and freshly ground black pepper
½ cup chopped fresh cilantro
3 cups cooked jasmine rice, hot

1. Soak beans in cold water to cover for a minimum of 6 hours, or preferably overnight. Or place beans in a saucepan covered with water, and bring to a boil over high heat. Boil for 1 minute, turn off the heat, and cover the pan. Allow beans to soak for 1 hour, then drain. With either method, continue with the dish as soon as beans have soaked, or refrigerate beans.

*Available in the Asian aisle of most supermarkets and in specialty markets.

2. Heat sesame oil in a 4-quart saucepan over medium-high heat. Add scallions, garlic, and ginger, and cook for 30 seconds, stirring constantly. Add turkey, and cook for 3 minutes, breaking up lumps with a fork. Add beans, stock, sherry, hoisin sauce, soy sauce, vinegar, black bean sauce, chile paste, and sugar, and bring to a boil over high heat, stirring occasionally.
3. Reduce the heat to low, and cook mixture, covered, for 45–55 minutes, or until beans are tender. Season to taste with salt and pepper, and stir in cilantro. Serve immediately over rice.

Note: The dish can be prepared up to 2 days in advance and refrigerated, tightly covered. Reheat it, covered, over low heat, stirring occasionally, until hot.

Variations:

- Substitute ground pork for the ground turkey.
- Substitute ground beef for the ground turkey, and substitute beef stock for the chicken stock.
- Substitute 1 pound zucchini, cut into 1-inch cubes, for the ground turkey, and substitute vegetable stock for the chicken stock, for a vegetarian stew.

Chapter 7:

Meaty Matters: Soups and Stews with Beef, Pork, and Lamb

Braising beef, pork, and lamb—the basis of the recipes in this chapter—makes tender, flavorful soups and stews that perfectly define "comfort foods."

No cuisine or culture can claim braising, although we've borrowed our English word from the French. While they may be called "sandpots" in China, "ragouts" in France, and "stews" in North America, every culture has less tender cuts of meat, which are usually also less expensive, that are simmered in aromatic liquid for many hours until they're tender.

That's what braising is all about—tenderness. And the amount of time it takes to reach the descriptive state of "fork tender" depends on each individual piece of meat; there are no hard and fast rules. That's why soups can take almost as long to cook as stews, and stews can take almost as long to cook as whole roasts.

Braising is a low heat method, since the meat is the same temperature as the simmering liquid, 212°F. This simmering converts the collagen of the meat's connective tissue to gelatin, tenderizing the meat.

PICKING YOUR PARTS

The best beef, in terms of both flavor and texture, comes from cows 18 to 24 months old. Beef is graded in the United States by the Department of Agriculture as Prime, Choice, or Select. Prime is usually reserved for restaurants, and the other two are found in supermarkets. Since the age, color, texture, and marbling are what determine the category, Prime beef is the most marbled and contains the most fat.

When you're looking at beef in the case, seek deep red, moist meat generously marbled with white fat. Yellow fat is a tip-off to old age. Beef is purple after cutting, but the meat quickly "blooms" to bright red on exposure to the air. Well-aged beef is dark and dry. To avoid paying for waste, be sure meat is thoroughly trimmed by a butcher. Otherwise a low per-pound price can translate into a higher cost for the edible portion.

You can usually save money by cutting the meat into cubes yourself. The general guideline is that if it's less expensive, then it's the cut you want, but here are some specifics:

- Chuck is the beef taken from between the neck and shoulder blades. Some chuck roasts also contain a piece of the blade bone, but it's easy to cull the meat from a chuck roast.

- Round is the general name for the large quantity of beef from the hind leg extending from the rump to the ankle. The eye of the round and the bottom round are the two least tender cuts, while the top round should be reserved for roasting.

PORKY PARTS

Pork has very little internal connective tissue and is inherently tender, because pigs don't wander and run around the prairies like cows and lambs. It is one of the few meats that can be equally good roasted or slowly braised in aromatic liquid. With the exception of pork shoulder, which is more muscular and fatty and should be cooked with liquid, almost all loin cuts can be done either way.

Pork has layers of fat that encircle the meat rather than marbling it. Some fat should be left on so that the meat does not dry out when cooking.

With the exception of the tenderloin, which will become stringy if subjected to long, slow cooking, almost all cuts of pork are up for grabs. That's why you don't find precut pork for stews the way that other animals' trimmings are packaged. Just choose pork that looks lean and is the least expensive.

The two best cuts of pork for soups and stews are boneless country ribs and boneless loin. Very often whole loins—usually about 10 pounds—are on sale for a very low price, so it is worth it to buy one and freeze most for future meals. Boneless country ribs, on the other hand, are the pork equivalent of a chuck roast; they have great flavor and become meltingly tender.

One warning regarding spare ribs is in order. While they're great on the grill, use only the boneless country ribs for braised dishes, because the percentage of bone to meat is so great that bone-in ribs require far too much liquid to cook.

CREATIVE CUTTING

Compared to the precision needed to cut a whole chicken into its component parts, boning and cutting meat for the recipes in this chapter is a free-for-all. The bones should be removed, however. Not only do they take up space needed for vegetables in your Dutch oven, but the bones slow down the cooking process, too, because they absorb heat and take it away from the meat. But do save any bones for making Beef Stock (recipe on page 24); unfortunately pork bones do not make a good stock.

The first step of trimming is to cut away the bones. Then cut away any large areas of fat that can be easily discarded. The last step is to decide how the remaining boneless meat should be cut. Read your recipe to determine how large the cubes should be.

The rule is to cut across the grain rather than with the grain. If you're not sure which way the grain runs, make a test slice. You should see the ends of fibers if you cut across the grain. The reason for this is that meat becomes more tender if the ends of the fibers are exposed to the liquid and heat.

PROCEDURAL PROWESS

The one major principle for almost all the recipes in this chapter is the initial browning of the meat, which means cooking the meat quickly over moderately high heat. This causes the surface of the food to brown. In the case of cubes of beef for stew, browning seals in the juices and keeps the interior moist; for ground meats, browning gives food an appetizing color, allows you to drain off some of the inherent fat, and also gives dishes a rich flavor.

While larger pieces can be browned under an oven broiler, ground meats are browned in a skillet. Crumble the meat in a skillet over medium-high heat. Break up the lumps with a meat fork or the back of a spoon as the meat browns, and then stir it around frequently until all lumps are brown and no pink remains. At that point, it's easy to remove the meat from the pan with a slotted spoon and discard the grease from the pan. You can then use the pan again without washing it for any precooking of other ingredients.

CUTTING THE CALORIES

In addition to cost, another benefit of braising meats is that it's possible to remove a great percentage of the saturated fat. It's easy to find and discard this "bad fat," both before and after cooking.

On raw meat, it's easy to spot. It's the white stuff around the red stuff. Cut it off with a sharp paring knife, and you're done.

While some fat remains in the tissue, much of the saturated fat is released during the cooking process, and there are ways to discard it both hot and cold. We'll start with the easiest thing: If you're cooking in advance and refrigerating a dish, all the fat rises to the top and hardens once chilled. Just scrape it off and throw it away.

The same principle of fat rising to the surface is true when food is hot, but it's a bit harder to eliminate it. Tilt the pan, and the fat will form a puddle on the lower side. It's then easier to scoop it off with a soup ladle. When you're down to too little to scoop off, level the pan, and blot the top with paper towels. You'll get even more fat off with this process.

Italian Beef and Bean Soup

This hearty soup made with a few types of canned beans is loaded with beefy flavor. Serve it with Basic Focaccia (recipe on page 222) or garlic bread, and a tossed green salad.

Yield: 4–6 servings | **Active time:** 20 minutes | **Start to finish:** 1½ hours

¾ pound boneless chuck roast, trimmed and cut into ¾-inch dice
Salt and freshly ground black pepper to taste
2 tablespoons olive oil
1 large onion, peeled and diced
2 garlic cloves, peeled and minced
1 carrot, peeled and diced
5 cups Beef Stock (recipe on page 24) or purchased stock
1 (14.5-ounce) can diced tomatoes, petite cut if possible, undrained
1 tablespoon tomato paste
2 tablespoons chopped fresh parsley
1 bay leaf
1 teaspoon Italian seasoning
1 (15-ounce) can red kidney beans, drained and rinsed
1 (15-ounce) can white cannellini beans, drained and rinsed

1. Rinse beef and pat dry with paper towels. Sprinkle beef with salt and pepper.
2. Heat oil in a 4-quart saucepan over medium-high heat. Add beef, and brown well on all sides. Remove beef from the pan with a slotted spoon, and set aside. Add onion, garlic, and carrot to the pan, and cook, stirring frequently, for 3 minutes, or until onion is translucent.
3. Return beef to the pan, and add stock, tomatoes, tomato paste, parsley, bay leaf, and Italian seasoning, and stir well to dissolve tomato paste. Bring to a boil over medium-high heat, reduce the heat to low, and simmer soup, covered, for 40 minutes.
4. Add kidney beans and cannellini beans, and simmer for an additional 20–30 minutes, or until beef is tender. Remove and discard bay leaf, season to taste with salt and pepper, and serve immediately.

Note: The soup can be prepared up to 2 days in advance and refrigerated, tightly covered. Reheat it over low heat, covered, until hot, stirring occasionally.

Variations:

- Substitute vegetable stock for the beef stock, and add an additional (15-ounce) can of beans, drained and rinsed. Reduce the cooking time in Step 3 to 20 minutes.

Canned beans should always be added close to the end of the cooking time. They are already fully cooked, and if they're simmered for more than 30 minutes they can become mushy.

Chili Soup with Beans

This dish is a soup version of chili con carne. It has all the same seasonings, plus nutritious beans. Serve it with some warm corn or whole wheat tortillas, and a tossed salad.

Yield: 4–6 servings | **Active time:** 20 minutes | **Start to finish:** 1 hour

SOUP

3 tablespoons olive oil, divided
3/4 pound ground chuck
1 large onion, peeled and diced
1 large green bell pepper, seeds and ribs removed, diced
1 celery rib, rinsed, trimmed, and diced
3 garlic cloves, peeled and minced
2 tablespoons chili powder
2 teaspoons ground cumin
4 cups Beef Stock (recipe on page 24) or purchased stock
1 (14.5-ounce) can diced tomatoes, undrained
1 (4-ounce) can diced mild green chiles, drained
2 tablespoons tomato paste
2 (15-ounce) cans red kidney beans, drained and rinsed
Salt and freshly ground black pepper to taste

GARNISH

1/2–3/4 cup grated cheddar cheese
1/2–3/4 cup sour cream or plain yogurt
1/4–1/2 cup diced onion

1. Heat 1 tablespoon oil in a 4-quart saucepan over medium-high heat. Add beef, breaking up lumps with a fork, and cook for 2–3 minutes, or until beef browns and no pink remains. Remove beef from the pan with a slotted spoon, and set aside. Discard fat from the pan.
2. Heat remaining 2 tablespoons oil over medium-high heat. Add onion, green bell pepper, celery, and garlic. Cook, stirring frequently, for 3 minutes, or until onion is translucent. Add chili powder and cumin, and cook for 1 minute, stirring constantly.

3. Return beef to the pan and add stock, tomatoes, chiles, and tomato paste. Stir well to dissolve tomato paste, and bring to a boil over medium-high heat.
4. Reduce the heat to low, and simmer soup, covered, for 20 minutes. Add beans, and cook for an additional 20 minutes. Season to taste with salt and pepper, and serve immediately, passing bowls of cheddar, sour cream, and onion separately.

Note: The soup can be prepared up to 2 days in advance and refrigerated, tightly covered. Reheat it over low heat, covered, until hot, stirring occasionally.

Variation:

- Substitute ground turkey for the ground beef, and substitute chicken stock for the beef stock.

Be careful when pushing your shopping cart up the Mexican aisle that what you're buying are mild green chiles and not canned jalapeño chiles. The cans are always next to each other, and the mistake turns this mildly flavored dish into one needing a fire extinguisher.

Beef and Beet Borscht

Roasting beets intensifies their innate sweetness, and it also turns this traditional Eastern European soup a bright crimson red. Serve it with a loaf of crusty rye bread or pumpernickel, along with a cabbage salad.

Yield: 4–6 servings | **Active time:** 25 minutes | **Start to finish:** 2½ hours

1¾ pounds fresh beets
¾ pound boneless chuck roast, trimmed and cut into ¾-inch dice
Salt and freshly ground black pepper to taste
2 tablespoons vegetable oil
1 large onion, peeled and diced
1 carrot, peeled and chopped
2 garlic cloves, peeled and minced
4 cups firmly packed shredded green cabbage
4 cups Beef Stock (recipe on page 24) or purchased stock
1 (14.5-ounce) can diced tomatoes, undrained
2 tablespoons chopped fresh parsley
¾ pound redskin potatoes, scrubbed and cut into 1-inch cubes
2 tablespoons lemon juice
2 tablespoons granulated sugar
½–¾ cup sour cream

1. Preheat the oven to 425°F. Cut leaves off beets, leaving stem attached. Scrub beets gently, and wrap them in a double layer of heavy-duty aluminum foil. Place foil packet on a baking sheet, and bake beets for 1–1¼ hours, or until tender when pierced with the tip of a knife. When beets are cool enough to handle, peel and cut into ½-inch dice.
2. While beets roast, rinse beef and pat dry with paper towels. Sprinkle beef with salt and pepper.
3. Heat oil in a 4-quart saucepan over medium-high heat. Add beef, and brown well on all sides. Remove beef from the pan with a slotted spoon, and set aside. Add onion, carrot, and garlic to the pan, and cook, stirring frequently, for 3 minutes, or until onion is translucent. Add cabbage, and cook for 2 minutes, or until cabbage wilts.

4. Return beef to the pan, and add stock, tomatoes, and parsley. Bring to a boil over medium-high heat, reduce the heat to low, and simmer soup, covered, for 1½ hours; add beets to the pan when they are ready.
5. Add potatoes, lemon juice, and sugar to the pan, and boil for an additional 30 minutes, or until beef and potatoes are tender. Season to taste with salt and pepper, and serve immediately, garnishing each serving with sour cream.

Note: The soup can be prepared up to 2 days in advance and refrigerated, tightly covered. Reheat it over low heat, covered, until hot, stirring occasionally.

Variation:

- Omit the beef, and substitute vegetable stock for the beef stock for a vegetarian dish.

The pigment that gives beets their rich, purple-crimson color—betacyanin—is also a powerful cancer-fighting agent. Beets' potential effectiveness against colon cancer, in particular, has been demonstrated in several studies. They are also high in manganese and folate.

Classic Onion Soup with Beef

Could there be a more quintessential comfort food soup than this? Sweet caramelized onions and beef in a richly flavored broth are topped with a cheese-encrusted slice of toast. Serve it with a green salad.

Yield: 4–6 servings | **Active time:** 20 minutes | **Start to finish:** 2½ hours

- 4 tablespoons (½ stick) unsalted butter
- ¼ cup olive oil
- 3 pounds sweet onions, such as Vidalia or Bermuda, peeled, halved, and thinly sliced
- 1 tablespoon granulated sugar
- Salt and freshly ground black pepper to taste
- 3 tablespoons all-purpose flour
- 1 pound boneless chuck roast, trimmed and cut into ¾-inch cubes
- 5½ cups Beef Stock (recipe on page 24) or purchased stock
- ¾ cup dry red wine
- 3 tablespoons chopped fresh parsley
- 1 bay leaf
- 1 teaspoon dried thyme
- 4–6 slices French or Italian bread, cut 1 inch thick
- ⅓ cup freshly grated Parmesan cheese
- 1½ cups grated Gruyère or Swiss cheese

1. Melt butter and oil in a large skillet over medium heat. Add onions, sugar, salt, and pepper, and toss to coat onions. Cover the skillet, and cook for 10 minutes, stirring occasionally. Uncover the skillet, and cook over medium-high heat for 20–30 minutes, or until onions are browned. Stir in flour, reduce the heat to low, and cook for 2 minutes, stirring constantly. Transfer onions to a 4-quart saucepan.
2. While onions cook, preheat the oven broiler, and line a broiler pan with heavy-duty aluminum foil. Rinse beef and pat dry with paper towels. Broil beef for 3 minutes per side, or until browned. Add beef, stock, wine, parsley, bay leaf, and thyme to the saucepan with the onions. Bring to a boil over medium-high heat, stirring occasionally. Reduce the heat to low, and simmer soup, covered, for 1–1½ hours, or until beef is tender.

3. While soup cooks, preheat the oven to 450°F, and cover a baking sheet with aluminum foil. Sprinkle bread with Parmesan cheese, and bake slices for 5–8 minutes, or until browned. Remove, and set aside.
4. Preheat the oven broiler. Remove and discard bay leaf from soup, and season soup to taste with salt and pepper. To serve, ladle hot soup into ovenproof soup bowls and top each with toast slice. Sprinkle Gruyère on top of toast and broil 6 inches from heating element for 1–2 minutes, or until cheese melts and browns. Serve immediately.

Note: The soup can be made up to 2 days in advance and refrigerated, tightly covered. Reheat it over low heat, covered, until hot, stirring occasionally. The toasts can be made up to 2 days in advance and kept at room temperature. Do not top with cheese and broil until just before serving.

Variation:

- Omit the beef, and substitute vegetable stock for the beef stock. Reduce the cooking time to 45 minutes.

If you don't have ovenproof soup bowls, you can still enjoy the gooey toast topping. Arrange the toast slices on a baking sheet lined with aluminum foil, and top with the cheese. Broil until the cheese melts, and then transfer the toasts to soup bowls with a wide spatula.

Two Mushroom, Beef, and Barley Soup

The combination of beef and woodsy mushrooms make this soup a satisfying winter treat, and the healthful barley thickens the soup as well as adding its nutty flavor.

Yield: 6–8 servings | **Active time:** 20 minutes | **Start to finish:** 1½ hours

¼ cup dried mushrooms, such as porcini
½ cup boiling water
¾ pound boneless chuck roast, trimmed and cut into ¾-inch dice
2 tablespoons olive oil
1 large onion, peeled and diced
2 carrots, peeled and sliced
2 celery ribs, rinsed, trimmed, and sliced
1 pound white mushrooms, rinsed, stemmed, and sliced
6 cups Beef Stock (recipe on page 24) or purchased stock
¾ cup pearl barley, rinsed well
3 tablespoons chopped fresh parsley
1 teaspoon dried thyme
Salt and freshly ground black pepper to taste

1. Combine dried mushrooms and boiling water, pushing the mushrooms down into the water. Soak for 10 minutes, then drain mushrooms, reserving soaking liquid, and chop mushrooms. Strain soaking liquid through a sieve lined with a paper coffee filter or a paper towel. Set aside.
2. Rinse beef, and pat dry with paper towels. Heat oil in a 3-quart saucepan over medium-high heat. Add beef and brown well on all sides. Remove beef from the pan with a slotted spoon, and set aside. Add onion and cook, stirring frequently, for 3 minutes, or until onion is translucent.
3. Return beef to the pan, and add carrots, celery, white mushrooms, stock, barley, parsley, thyme, chopped dried mushroom, and reserved mushroom liquid. Bring to a boil over medium-high heat. Reduce the heat to low, and simmer soup, covered, for 1 hour, or until beef and barley are tender. Season to taste with salt and pepper, and serve hot.

Note: The soup can be prepared up to 2 days in advance and refrigerated, tightly covered. Reheat it over low heat, covered, until hot, stirring occasionally.

Variation:

- For the ultimate in mushroom flavor, substitute fresh portobello mushrooms for the white mushrooms if you can find them on sale.

> If you have an egg slicer, use it for slicing the mushrooms. That way they're all the same width.

Irish Ham and Cabbage Soup

I'm always looking for ways to use up leftover baked ham, and this hearty soup is a delicious answer. Serve it with a salad and Irish Soda Bread (recipe on page 228).

Yield: 4–6 servings | **Active time:** 20 minutes | **Start to finish:** 45 minutes

3 tablespoons unsalted butter
1 large onion, peeled and chopped
3 cups firmly packed shredded green cabbage
1 carrot, peeled and chopped
1 celery rib, rinsed, trimmed, and chopped
6 cups Chicken Stock (recipe on page 23) or purchased stock
2 large redskin potatoes, scrubbed and cut into $3/4$-inch dice
$1/4$ cup chopped fresh parsley
2 bay leaves
1 teaspoon dried thyme
$2/3$ pound baked ham, trimmed and cut into $1/2$-inch dice
Salt and freshly ground black pepper to taste

1. Heat butter in a 4-quart saucepan over medium heat. Add onion, and cook, stirring frequently, for 2 minutes. Add cabbage, carrot, and celery, and cook for 3 minutes, or until onion is translucent and cabbage wilts.
2. Add stock, potatoes, parsley, bay leaves, and thyme. Bring to a boil over medium-high heat, stirring occasionally. Reduce the heat to medium, and simmer soup, partially covered, for 10–12 minutes, or until vegetables are tender. Remove and discard bay leaves.
3. With a slotted spoon, transfer 1 cup of solids to a food processor fitted with the steel blade or to a blender. Be careful not to fill the beaker too full when blending hot ingredients. Puree until smooth, and return mixture to the saucepan.
4. Bring soup back to a simmer over medium-high heat, stirring occasionally. Add ham, and cook over low heat for 5 minutes. Season to taste with salt and pepper, and serve immediately.

Note: The soup can be prepared up to 2 days in advance and refrigerated, tightly covered. Reheat it over low heat, covered, until hot, stirring occasionally.

Variation:

- Substitute corned beef for the ham.

The English word cabbage comes from the French *caboche,* which means "head." While we associate cabbage with Europe, especially Ireland, the vegetable is actually native to Asia. It was brought to Europe by the Celts about 600 B.C.E.

Gumbo Z'herbes

This traditional Cajun gumbo is made with ham and a number of fresh greens. Greens are extremely high in nutrients, and their bitter flavor is a great contrast with the salty ham. Serve this over rice, with a bowl of coleslaw on the side.

Yield: 4–6 servings | **Active time:** 30 minutes | **Start to finish:** 1 hour

- 1/3 cup vegetable oil
- 2/3 cup all-purpose flour
- 3 tablespoons unsalted butter
- 1 large onion, peeled and diced
- 2 celery ribs, rinsed, trimmed, and diced
- 5 garlic cloves, peeled and minced
- 2 tablespoons filé powder
- 4 cups Chicken Stock (recipe on page 23) or purchased stock, divided
- 4 cups sliced collard greens, rinsed well
- 4 cups sliced mustard greens, rinsed well
- 1/2 cup chopped fresh parsley
- 1 teaspoon dried thyme
- 2 bay leaves
- 3/4 pound baked ham, trimmed and cut into 1/2-inch dice
- Hot red pepper sauce to taste
- Salt and freshly ground black pepper to taste
- 3 cups cooked brown or white rice, hot

1. Preheat the oven to 450°F. Combine oil and flour in a Dutch oven, and place the pan in the oven. Bake roux for 20–30 minutes, or until walnut brown, stirring occasionally.
2. While roux bakes, melt butter in large skillet over medium-high heat. Add onion, celery, and garlic. Cook, stirring frequently, for 3 minutes, or until onion is translucent. Add filé powder, and cook for 30 seconds, stirring constantly. Add 1 1/2 cups stock, collard greens, mustard greens, parsley, thyme, and bay leaves. Bring to a boil over medium-high heat, then cover the pan and cook, covered, over low heat for 12–15 minutes, or until greens are tender.

3. Remove and discard bay leaves. Transfer mixture to a food processor fitted with the steel blade or to a blender. Be careful not to fill the beaker too full when blending hot ingredients. Puree until smooth.
4. Remove roux from oven, and place the pan on the stove over medium heat. Whisk in remaining 2½ cups stock, and whisk constantly, until mixture comes to a boil and thickens. Add vegetable puree and ham, and cook for an additional 10 minutes.
5. Season to taste with hot red pepper sauce, salt, and pepper. Serve immediately over rice.

Note: The soup can be prepared up to 2 days in advance and refrigerated, tightly covered. Reheat it over low heat, covered, until hot, stirring occasionally.

Variation:

- Substitute andouille or other hot smoked sausage for the ham. Brown the sausage with the onions.

Filé is a powder made from ground sassafras leaves that serves as an alternative to okra for thickening gumbo. It's available in the spice section of most supermarkets.

Tuscan White Bean Soup with Sausage

This hearty soup is relatively fast to make because I developed the recipe using canned beans that require no soaking. The combination of the mild beans with the hearty sausage is delicious, and a tossed salad is all you need to complete the meal.

Yield: 4–6 servings | **Active time:** 20 minutes | **Start to finish:** 45 minutes

- 2/3 pound bulk Italian sausage (sweet or hot)
- 2 medium onions, peeled and diced
- 3 garlic cloves, peeled and minced
- 2 celery ribs, rinsed, trimmed, and diced
- 1 large carrot, peeled and diced
- 1 (6-inch) rind from Parmesan cheese (optional)
- 3 cups Chicken Stock (recipe on page 23) or purchased stock
- 2 (15-ounce) cans white beans, drained and rinsed, divided
- 1/4 cup chopped fresh parsley
- 1 teaspoon dried thyme
- 1 bay leaf
- 3/4 cup water
- 1/2 pound Swiss chard, rinsed, stemmed, and thinly sliced
- 1/2 cup freshly grated Parmesan cheese
- Salt and freshly ground black pepper to taste

1. Place a heavy 4-quart saucepan over medium-high heat. Add sausage, breaking up lumps with a fork. Cook, stirring frequently, for 3–5 minutes, or until sausage is browned and no longer pink. Remove sausage from the pan with a slotted spoon, and set aside. Discard all but 2 tablespoons sausage fat from the pan.
2. Add onion, garlic, celery, and carrot to the pan. Cook for 3 minutes, stirring frequently, or until onion is translucent. Add sausage, Parmesan rind (if using), stock, 1 can beans, parsley, thyme, and bay leaf to the pan. Bring to a boil over medium heat, and simmer, partially covered, for 20 minutes, or until carrots are soft.
3. While soup simmers, combine reserved can of beans and water in a blender or food processor fitted with the steel blade. Puree until smooth, and stir mixture into soup.

4. Add Swiss chard to soup, and simmer for 5 minutes. Remove and discard bay leaf and Parmesan rind (if using), and stir Parmesan cheese into soup. Season to taste with salt and pepper, and serve immediately.

Note: The soup can be prepared up to 2 days in advance and refrigerated, tightly covered. Reheat it over low heat, covered, until hot, stirring occasionally.

Variation:

- Substitute ground pork or ground beef for the sausage for a soup with a milder flavor.

> Remember, in my kitchen nothing goes to waste! So I save the rinds from Parmesan cheese and use them for flavoring dishes such as soups and sauces. The rind will not melt into the dishes, but it will impart flavor. Remove and discard it before serving.

Guinness Beef Stew

This is a heartier version of the classic Belgian dish *Carbonnades à la Flamande,* which is beef cooked in a light beer. It's traditionally served with steamed potatoes, but I like roasted potatoes to provide some textural contrast.

Yield: 4–6 servings | **Active time:** 20 minutes | **Start to finish:** 3 hours

1 (2-pound) chuck roast, trimmed and cut into 1-inch cubes, or 1½ pounds stewing beef
3 tablespoons vegetable oil
4 large onions, peeled and thinly sliced
2 garlic cloves, peeled and minced
2 teaspoons granulated sugar
Salt to taste
1½ cups Beef Stock (recipe on page 24) or purchased stock
1 (12-ounce) bottle Guinness stout beer
2 tablespoons firmly packed dark brown sugar
2 tablespoons chopped fresh parsley
1 teaspoon dried thyme
1 bay leaf
1 tablespoon cornstarch
1 tablespoon cold water
Freshly ground black pepper to taste

1. Preheat the oven broiler, and line a broiler pan with heavy-duty aluminum foil. Rinse beef and pat dry with paper towels. Arrange beef in a single layer on the foil, and broil for 3 minutes per side, or until beef is lightly browned. Preheat the oven to 350°F.
2. Heat oil in a Dutch oven over medium heat. Add onions and garlic, toss to coat with fat, and cook, covered, for 10 minutes. Uncover the pan, raise the heat to medium-high, and sprinkle onions with granulated sugar and salt. Cook, stirring occasionally, for 10–12 minutes, or until onions are lightly browned.
3. Add beef to the pan, and stir in stock, beer, brown sugar, parsley, thyme, and bay leaf. Bring to a boil on top of the stove, stirring occasionally.

4. Cover the pan, and bake for 2–2½ hours, or until meat is tender. Spoon off as much fat as possible from surface. Remove and discard bay leaf. Combine cornstarch and water in a small cup, and stir into stew. Cook over low heat for 1–2 minutes, or until slightly thickened. Season to taste with salt and pepper, and serve immediately.

Note: The dish can be made up to 2 days in advance and refrigerated, tightly covered. Reheat it over low heat or in a 350°F oven for 30 minutes, or until hot.

Variation:

- Substitute lager beer for the Guinness stout. The stew will have a less hearty flavor.

While beer usually doesn't work as a beverage when food is cooked in wine, the reverse is not valid. While you can serve this stew with additional Guinness stout, a rich red wine also pairs nicely.

Beef Stroganoff Stew

Beef Stroganoff was named for a nineteenth-century Russian diplomat, Count Paul Stroganoff; it became a hallmark of what Americans called "continental cuisine" in the mid-twentieth century. While the original Beef Stroganoff is a quickly sautéed dish, this long-simmered braise has the same flavors of sour cream and rich tomato sauce.

Yield: 4–6 servings | **Active time:** 15 minutes | **Start to finish:** 3 hours

- 1 (2-pound) chuck roast, trimmed and cut into 1-inch cubes, or 1½ pounds stewing beef
- Salt and freshly ground black pepper to taste
- ½ cup all-purpose flour
- 3 tablespoons vegetable oil
- 2 tablespoons unsalted butter
- 2 large onions, peeled and diced
- 2 garlic cloves, peeled and minced
- ½ pound mushrooms, wiped with a damp paper towel, trimmed, and sliced
- 2 tablespoons paprika
- 2 cups Beef Stock (recipe on page 24) or purchased stock
- 3 tablespoons tomato paste
- 2 tablespoons chopped fresh parsley
- 1 tablespoon Dijon mustard
- ½ cup sour cream

1. Preheat the oven to 350°F. Rinse beef and pat dry with paper towels. Season beef with salt and pepper, and dust with flour, shaking off excess over the sink or a garbage can.
2. Heat oil in a Dutch oven over medium-high heat. Add beef, and cook, turning pieces with tongs, until brown on all sides. Remove meat from the pan with a slotted spoon, and set aside.
3. Add butter to the pan. When butter melts, add onion and garlic, and cook, stirring frequently, for 3 minutes, or until onion is translucent. Add mushrooms, and cook for 2 minutes more. Add paprika to the pan, and cook for 1 minute, stirring constantly.
4. Add stock, tomato paste, parsley, and mustard to the pan. Stir well, return meat to the pan, and bring to a boil on top of the stove, stirring occasionally.

5. Cover the pan, and bake for 2–2½ hours, or until meat is tender. Spoon off as much fat as possible from surface. Stir in sour cream, and season to taste with salt and pepper. *Do not allow dish to boil.* Serve immediately.

Note: The dish can be made up to 2 days in advance and refrigerated, tightly covered. Reheat it over low heat or in a 350°F oven for 30 minutes, or until hot.

Variation:

- Make the dish with boneless, skinless chicken thighs, and reduce the cooking time to 1½–2 hours.

> Sauces made with sour cream shouldn't be allowed to boil because the sour cream will curdle. A similar product on the market, French crème fraîche, does not curdle, but it's quite expensive compared to sour cream. But you can make it yourself. Combine 1 cup heavy cream with 3 tablespoons plain yogurt or sour cream, and allow it to sit at room temperature for 18–24 hours, or until thickened.

Beef Braised in Red Wine with Potatoes and Vegetables (*Boeuf Bourguignon*)

While cooking with wine is more expensive than cooking with stock, a "cooking wine" hardly needs to be of high quality; forget the old adage that "you never cook with a wine you wouldn't drink." This hearty stew is perfect for a fall or winter night.

Yield: 4–6 servings | **Active time:** 20 minutes | **Start to finish:** 3 hours

- 1 (2-pound) chuck roast, trimmed and cut into 1-inch cubes, or 1½ pounds stewing beef
- Salt and freshly ground black pepper to taste
- ½ cup all-purpose flour
- ¼ cup olive oil
- 1 large onion, peeled and diced
- 3 garlic cloves, peeled and minced
- ½ pound small mushrooms, wiped with a damp paper towel, trimmed, and halved if large
- 2 cups dry red wine
- 1 cup Beef Stock (recipe on page 24) or purchased stock
- 2 tablespoons tomato paste
- 2 tablespoons chopped fresh parsley
- 2 teaspoons herbes de Provence
- 1 bay leaf
- 2 carrots, peeled and cut into 1-inch chunks
- 1 pound baby red potatoes, scrubbed, or small red potatoes cut into quarters

1. Preheat the oven to 350°F. Rinse beef and pat dry with paper towels. Season beef with salt and pepper, and dust with flour, shaking off excess over the sink or a garbage can.
2. Heat oil in a Dutch oven over medium-high heat. Add beef, and cook, turning pieces with tongs, until brown on all sides. Remove beef from the pan with a slotted spoon, and set aside.
3. Add onion and garlic to the pan, and cook, stirring frequently, for 3 minutes, or until onion is translucent. Add mushrooms, and cook for 2 minutes more. Add wine, stock, tomato paste, parsley, herbes de Provence, and bay leaf to the pan. Stir well, return meat to the pan, and bring to a boil on top of the stove, stirring occasionally.

4. Cover the pan, transfer it to the oven, and bake for 1 hour. Remove the pan from the oven, add carrots and potatoes, and return it to the oven for an additional 1½ hours, or until meat and potatoes are tender. Spoon off as much fat as possible from surface, remove and discard bay leaf, and serve immediately.

Note: The dish can be made up to 2 days in advance and refrigerated, tightly covered. Reheat it over low heat or in a 350°F oven for 30 minutes, or until hot.

> Food that will be browned in oil is often coated with flour to produce an appetizing brown skin. The proteins in the flour are cooked so they'll lightly thicken the pan juices with no "floury" taste. Some sort of fat like butter or oil is necessary when browning flour, which is why stews and roasts browned under the broiler are thickened most often with cornstarch.

Braised Beef with Rosemary and Celery

Aromatic rosemary and delicate celery transform this stew into a lighter, and more elegant, dish. Serve it with some buttered egg noodles or steamed potatoes, and a green vegetable.

Yield: 4–6 servings | **Active time:** 20 minutes | **Start to finish:** 3 hours

- 1 (2-pound) chuck roast, trimmed and cut into 1-inch cubes, or 1½ pounds stewing beef
- Salt and freshly ground black pepper to taste
- ½ cup all-purpose flour
- 3 tablespoons olive oil
- 2 large onions, peeled and diced
- 6 celery ribs, rinsed, trimmed, and sliced
- 4 garlic cloves, peeled and minced
- 2 cups Beef Stock (recipe on page 24) or purchased stock
- 3 tablespoons chopped fresh rosemary or 1 tablespoon dried rosemary

1. Preheat the oven to 350°F. Rinse beef and pat dry with paper towels. Season beef with salt and pepper, and dust with flour, shaking off excess over the sink or a garbage can.
2. Heat oil in a Dutch oven over medium-high heat. Add beef and cook, turning with tongs, until browned on all sides. Remove beef from the pan with a slotted spoon, and add onions, celery, and garlic. Cook, stirring frequently, for 3 minutes, or until onions are translucent.
3. Return beef to the pan, and add stock and rosemary. Bring to a boil on top of the stove, then transfer to the oven, and bake for 2–2½ hours, or until the beef is fork tender.
4. Remove beef to a warm platter and tip the Dutch oven to spoon off as much grease as possible. Cook sauce over medium heat until reduced by ½. Season sauce to taste with salt and pepper, then pour sauce over beef, and serve immediately.

Note: Prepare this dish up to 2 days in advance and refrigerate. Reheat it, covered, in a 350°F oven for 25–35 minutes or until hot.

Variation:

- Substitute fennel for the celery, and substitute fresh oregano for the rosemary.

Sauerbraten Stew

Sauerbraten is the classic German pot roast, but I like to make it as a stew because the wonderful ginger flavor permeates all through the meat. Serve it with buttered egg noodles and a steamed green vegetable.

Yield: 4–6 servings | **Active time:** 15 minutes | **Start to finish:** 26¾ hours, including 24 hours to marinate meat

- 1 cup dry red wine
- 1 cup Beef Stock (recipe on page 24) or purchased stock
- ½ cup red wine vinegar
- ¼ cup firmly packed dark brown sugar
- 2 tablespoons tomato paste
- 2 tablespoons Worcestershire sauce
- 2 tablespoons Dijon mustard
- 1 teaspoon ground ginger
- Salt and freshly ground black pepper to taste
- 1 onion, peeled, halved, and thinly sliced
- 3 garlic cloves, peeled and thinly sliced
- 1 (2-pound) chuck roast, trimmed and cut into 1-inch cubes, or 1½ pounds stewing beef
- ½ cup water
- ⅔ cup crushed gingersnap cookies

1. Combine wine, stock, vinegar, brown sugar, tomato paste, Worcestershire sauce, mustard, and ginger in a heavy resealable plastic bag. Season to taste with salt and pepper. Mix well, and add onion, garlic, and beef. Marinate, refrigerated, for at least 24 hours, and up to 48 hours, turning the bag occasionally.
2. Preheat the oven to 350°F. Combine beef with its marinade, water, and crushed cookies in a Dutch oven. Bring to a boil on top of the stove, and then bake, covered, for 2½ hours, or until beef is tender. Serve immediately.

Note: The dish can be prepared up to 2 days in advance and refrigerated, tightly covered. Reheat it, covered, in a 350°F oven for 20–25 minutes, or until hot.

Hungarian Beef Goulash

Beef goulash, characterized by paprika and sour cream in a tomato sauce, has been around since the ninth century. Serve it over buttered egg noodles with a steamed green vegetable.

Yield: 4–6 servings | **Active time:** 20 minutes | **Start to finish:** 2¾ hours

1 (2-pound) chuck roast, trimmed and cut into 1-inch cubes, or 1½ pounds stewing beef
Salt and freshly ground black pepper to taste
½ cup all-purpose flour
2 tablespoons olive oil
1 tablespoon unsalted butter
1 large onion, peeled and diced
3 garlic cloves, peeled and minced
¼ cup paprika, preferably Hungarian
2 tablespoons tomato paste
2 cups Beef Stock (recipe on page 24) or purchased stock
2 carrots, peeled and cut into 1-inch chunks
3 celery ribs, rinsed, trimmed, and cut into 1-inch lengths
1 (10-ounce) package frozen cut green beans, thawed
1 cup sour cream
¼ cup chopped fresh dill (optional)

1. Preheat the oven to 350°F. Rinse meat and pat dry with paper towels. Season meat to taste with salt and pepper. Dust meat with flour, shaking off any excess into the sink or a garbage can. Heat oil and butter in a Dutch oven over medium-high heat. Add beef, and cook, turning pieces with tongs, until brown on all sides. Remove beef from the pan with a slotted spoon, and set aside.
2. Add onion and garlic to the Dutch oven and cook, stirring frequently, for 3 minutes, or until onion is translucent. Stir in paprika and cook for 1 minute, stirring constantly. Stir in tomato paste and stock, and bring to a boil over medium-high heat, stirring occasionally. Return beef to the pan, and bring to a boil over medium-high heat. Cover the pan, and place the pan in the oven. Cook 1 hour.
3. Add carrots and celery, and bake for an additional 1 hour. Add green beans, and bake for an additional 10–15 minutes, or until beef and vegetables are tender.

4. Return the Dutch oven to the top of the stove, and stir in sour cream. Heat the mixture over low heat, but do not let liquid boil. Season to taste with salt and pepper, and serve immediately, sprinkling each serving with dill, if using.

Note: The dish can be prepared up to 2 days in advance and refrigerated, tightly covered. Reheat it, covered, in a 350°F oven for 20–25 minutes, or until hot.

Variation:

- Substitute cubes of boneless pork loin for the beef, and reduce the initial baking time to 45 minutes.

> Paprika is a powder made by grinding aromatic sweet red pepper pods several times. The color can vary from deep red to bright orange, and the flavor ranges from mild to pungent and hot. Hungarian cuisine is characterized by paprika as a flavoring, and Hungarian paprika is considered the best product.

Mexican Beef Stew with Beans

Here is a hearty and somewhat spicy beef dish with great Mexican flavors. Serve it over rice with a tossed salad, and any leftover meat can be used for burritos or nachos.

Yield: 4–6 servings | **Active time:** 20 minutes | **Start to finish:** 2¾ hours

- 1 (2-pound) chuck roast, trimmed and cut into 1-inch cubes, or 1½ pounds stewing beef
- Salt and freshly ground black pepper to taste
- ½ cup all-purpose flour
- ¼ cup olive oil
- 1 large onion, peeled and diced
- 3 garlic cloves, peeled and minced
- 1 teaspoon ground cumin
- 1 teaspoon dried oregano
- 1–2 canned chipotle chiles in adobo sauce, finely chopped
- 2 cups Beef Stock (recipe on page 24) or purchased stock
- 1 (14.5-ounce) can diced tomatoes, undrained
- 1 (15-ounce) can red kidney beans, drained and rinsed
- 1 (10-ounce) package frozen corn, thawed
- ¼ cup chopped fresh cilantro (optional)
- 3 cups cooked brown or white rice, hot

1. Preheat the oven to 350°F. Season meat to taste with salt and pepper. Dust meat with flour, shaking off any excess into the sink or a garbage can.
2. Heat oil in a Dutch oven over medium-high heat. Add beef, and cook, turning pieces with tongs, until brown on all sides. Remove beef from the pan with a slotted spoon, and set aside.
3. Add onion and garlic to the Dutch oven and cook, stirring frequently, for 3 minutes, or until onion is translucent. Add cumin and oregano to the pan, and cook for 1 minute, stirring constantly. Return meat to the pan, and add chiles, stock, and tomatoes. Bring to a boil, cover the pan, and bake for 1½ hours.
4. Remove the pan from the oven, and add beans and corn. Bake for an additional 25–30 minutes, or until beef is tender. Season to taste with salt and pepper, and serve immediately, sprinkling each serving with cilantro, if using.

Note: The dish can be prepared up to 2 days in advance and refrigerated, tightly covered. Reheat it, covered, in a 350°F oven for 20–25 minutes, or until hot.

Variations:

- Substitute 1 (4-ounce) can diced mild green chiles for the chipotle chiles, for a milder dish.
- Add 1½ cups long-grain white rice to the stew along with the beans and corn, and bake for 40 minutes, or until rice is tender, adding more stock if necessary.

> While the cooking time for beef stews in the oven is the same as for cooking stew on top of the stove, if you want to convert an oven recipe to a stove-top recipe, increase the amount of liquid by ¾ cup because there is more evaporation on top of the stove.

Indian Beef Stew

This curried beef dish has a slightly sweet and sour flavor because mango chutney is part of the sauce. Serve it over some fragrant basmati rice, with a cucumber raita salad.

Yield: 4–6 servings | **Active time:** 20 minutes | **Start to finish:** 2¾ hours

- 1 (2-pound) chuck roast, trimmed and cut into 1-inch cubes, or 1½ pounds stewing beef
- Salt and freshly ground black pepper to taste
- 3 tablespoons vegetable oil
- 1 medium onion, peeled and diced
- 3 garlic cloves, peeled and minced
- 2 teaspoons curry powder
- ½ teaspoon ground ginger
- ½ cup jarred mango chutney
- ⅓ cup raisins
- 2 cups Beef Stock (recipe on page 24) or purchased stock
- 2 carrots, peeled and cut into ⅓-inch slices on the diagonal
- 2 celery ribs, rinsed, trimmed, and cut into ⅓-inch slices on the diagonal
- 1 (10-ounce) package frozen cut green beans, thawed
- 1 tablespoon cornstarch
- 2 tablespoons cold water
- 2–3 scallions, white parts and 4 inches of green tops, rinsed, trimmed, and thinly sliced (optional)
- 3 cups cooked basmati rice, hot

1. Preheat the oven to 350°F. Rinse beef and pat dry with paper towels. Season beef with salt and pepper.
2. Heat oil in a Dutch oven over medium-high heat. Add beef, and cook, turning pieces with tongs, until brown on all sides. Remove beef from the pan with a slotted spoon, and set aside.
3. Add onion and garlic to the pan, and cook, stirring frequently, for 3 minutes, or until onion is translucent. Stir in curry powder and ginger, and cook for 1 minute, stirring constantly. Stir in chutney, raisins, and stock. Return beef to the pan, and bring to a boil over medium-high heat. Cover the pan, and place the pan in the oven. Cook 1½ hours.

4. Add carrots and celery, and bake for an additional 30 minutes. Add green beans, and bake for an additional 10–15 minutes, or until beef and vegetables are tender.
5. Mix cornstarch with water in a small cup. Return the Dutch oven to the top of the stove, and stir in cornstarch mixture. Cook over medium heat, stirring frequently, for 2 minutes, or until liquid slightly thickens. Season to taste with salt and pepper, and serve immediately, sprinkling each serving with scallions, if using.

Note: The dish can be prepared up to 2 days in advance and refrigerated, tightly covered. Reheat it, covered, in a 350°F oven for 20–25 minutes, or until hot.

Variation:

- Substitute 1½ pounds boneless lamb shoulder, cut into 1-inch cubes, for the beef.

Chutney, from the Hindi word *chatni*, is a spicy Indian condiment containing some sort of fruit or vegetable, vinegar, and spices. It's always used as an accompaniment to curried dishes, but it can also be used with many foods to add a flavor accent.

Italian Pork Stew Bolognese

This stew has all the elements that define a true Bolognese sauce; it includes both milk and white wine along with vegetables and tomatoes. Serve it on top of either pasta or polenta, along with a green salad.

Yield: 4–6 servings | **Active time:** 15 minutes | **Start to finish:** 1¼ hours

1¼ pounds boneless pork loin, trimmed and cut into 1-inch cubes
Salt and freshly ground black pepper to taste
½ cup all-purpose flour
¼ cup olive oil
2 medium onions, peeled and diced
3 celery ribs, rinsed, trimmed, and diced
2 carrots, peeled and diced
4 garlic cloves, peeled and minced
1 (28-ounce) can diced tomatoes, undrained
½ cup whole milk
½ cup dry white wine
¼ cup chopped fresh parsley
1 tablespoon dried oregano
2 teaspoons dried thyme
1 bay leaf
½ cup freshly grated Parmesan cheese

1. Rinse pork and pat dry with paper towels. Season pork with salt and pepper, and dust with flour, shaking off excess over the sink or a garbage can.
2. Heat oil in a 3-quart saucepan over medium-high heat. Add pork, and cook, turning pieces with tongs, until brown on all sides. Remove pork from the pan with slotted spoon, and set aside.
3. Add onion, celery, carrots, and garlic to the pan, and cook, stirring frequently, for 3 minutes, or until onions are translucent. Return pork to the pan, and add tomatoes, milk, wine, parsley, oregano, thyme, and bay leaf.
4. Bring to a boil, reduce the heat to low, and simmer stew, partially covered and stirring occasionally, for 1¼–1½ hours, or until thickened and pork is tender. Remove and discard bay leaf. Stir in cheese, and season to taste with salt and pepper. Serve immediately.

Note: The dish can be prepared up to 2 days in advance and refrigerated, tightly covered. Reheat it, covered, in a 350°F oven for 20–25 minutes, or until hot.

Variation:

- Substitute boneless, skinless chicken thighs for the pork, and reduce the cooking time by 20 minutes.

> Partial covering of food while it simmers is the middle ground—when you want more evaporation than if a dish is covered and less evaporation than if it was uncovered. Uncovered pans need to be cooked over a higher flame, so the partial covering helps reduce scorching.

Chipotle Pork Stew

Here's a hearty pork stew dominated by spicy and smoky chipotle chiles, which are smoked jalapeño chiles. Serve this dish as a stew or transfer the pork to a cutting board. With two forks, shred the chunks into small pieces to use as a filling for tacos or sandwiches.

Yield: 4–6 servings | **Active time:** 20 minutes | **Start to finish:** 2 hours

1½ pounds boneless country pork ribs, cut into 1-inch cubes
Salt and freshly ground black pepper to taste
½ cup all-purpose flour
2 tablespoons olive oil
1 large onion, peeled and diced
3 garlic cloves, peeled and minced
2 tablespoons chili powder
2 teaspoons ground cumin
1 teaspoon dried oregano
1 (12-ounce) can or bottle beer
¾ cup Chicken Stock (recipe on page 23) or purchased stock
3–5 chipotle chiles in adobo sauce, finely chopped
2 tablespoons adobo sauce
2 large sweet potatoes, peeled and cut into 1-inch cubes
1 (10-ounce) package frozen mixed vegetables, thawed

1. Preheat the oven to 350°F. Rinse pork and pat dry with paper towels. Season pork with salt and pepper, and dust with flour, shaking off excess over the sink or a garbage can.
2. Heat oil in a Dutch oven over medium-high heat. Add pork, and cook, turning pieces with tongs, until brown on all sides. Remove pork from the pan with slotted spoon, and set aside.
3. Add onion and garlic to the pan, and cook, stirring frequently, for 3 minutes, or until onion is translucent. Add chili powder, cumin, and oregano, and cook for 1 minute, stirring constantly. Add beer, stock, chiles, and adobo sauce, and stir well.
4. Return pork to the pan and add sweet potatoes. Bring to a boil on top of the stove, stirring occasionally. Cover the pan, and bake for 1 hour. Remove the pan from the oven, add vegetables, and bake for an additional 30–40 minutes, or until meat and potatoes are tender. Season to taste with salt and pepper, and serve immediately.

Note: The dish can be prepared up to 2 days in advance and refrigerated, tightly covered. Reheat it, covered, in a 350°F oven for 20–25 minutes, or until hot.

Variation:

- Substitute beef for the pork and beef stock for the chicken stock. Cook beef for 1½ hours before adding mixed vegetables.

An alternative cut of pork for this, or any stewed pork dish, is a fresh ham, also called a picnic roast in some parts of the country. It has the same high fat content of boneless ribs.

Spicy Chinese Pork Stew

This is one of the fastest dishes to prepare because there's no need to brown the pork; it will absorb a wonderful color from the sauce. The dish is packed with pungent flavors from the fermented black beans and heady garlic, but it's not fiery spicy. While white rice is always appropriate, I'll sometimes serve it over angel hair pasta and transform it to a lo mein preparation.

Yield: 4–6 servings | **Active time:** 10 minutes | **Start to finish:** 1 hour

- 1½ pounds boneless country pork ribs, cut into 1-inch segments
- 6 scallions, white parts and 4 inches of green tops, rinsed, trimmed, and sliced
- 2 cups water
- ¼ cup dry sherry
- 5 tablespoons Chinese fermented black beans, coarsely chopped*
- 8 garlic cloves, peeled and minced
- 2 tablespoons soy sauce
- 2 tablespoons Asian sesame oil*
- 1 tablespoon firmly packed dark brown sugar
- 1 tablespoon cornstarch
- 1 tablespoon cold water
- Crushed red pepper flakes to taste
- 3 cups cooked brown or white rice, hot

1. Place pork and scallions in a 2-quart saucepan. Combine water, sherry, black beans, garlic, soy sauce, sesame oil, and brown sugar in a small bowl, and stir well. Pour mixture over ribs.
2. Bring to a boil over medium-high heat, stirring occasionally. Reduce the heat to low, cover the pan, and cook pork for 50–55 minutes, or until very tender. Mix cornstarch and water in a small cup, and stir mixture into stew. Cook for 1–2 minutes, or until slightly thickened, and season to taste with red pepper flakes. Serve immediately.

Note: The dish can be cooked up to 2 days in advance and refrigerated, tightly covered. Reheat it over low heat, covered, until hot, stirring occasionally.

*Available in the Asian aisle of most supermarkets and in specialty markets.

Variation:

- Substitute boneless, skinless chicken thighs for the pork; the cooking time will remain the same.

Fermented black beans are small black soybeans with a pungent flavor that have been preserved in salt before being packed. They should be chopped and soaked in some sort of liquid to soften them and release their flavor prior to cooking. Because they are salted as a preservative, they last for up to 2 years if refrigerated once opened.

Moroccan Lamb Stew with Dried Fruit

North African food includes a lot of lamb, as well as dried fruit and spices. Serve this stew over couscous to enjoy all the richly flavored sauce.

Yield: 4–6 servings | **Active time:** 20 minutes | **Start to finish:** 2¾ hours

1 (2-pound) boneless lamb shoulder, trimmed and cut into 1-inch cubes, or 1½ pounds lamb stew meat
Salt and freshly ground black pepper to taste
½ cup all-purpose flour
¼ cup olive oil
1 large onion, peeled and chopped
2 garlic cloves, peeled and minced
2½ cups Beef Stock (recipe on page 24) or purchased stock
1 teaspoon ground ginger
½ teaspoon ground cinnamon
¾ cup pitted prunes, diced
½ cup dried apricots, diced
2 large carrots, peeled and cut into ½-inch slices
1 large sweet potato, peeled and cut into ¾-inch dice
2 medium yellow squash, cut into ¾-inch dice
¼ cup chopped fresh cilantro (optional)

1. Preheat the oven to 350°F. Rinse lamb and pat dry with paper towels. Season lamb with salt and pepper, and dust with flour, shaking off excess over the sink or a garbage can.
2. Heat oil in a Dutch oven over medium-high heat. Add lamb, and cook, turning pieces with tongs, until brown on all sides. Remove lamb from the pan with a slotted spoon, and set aside.
3. Add onion and garlic to the Dutch oven and cook, stirring frequently, for 3 minutes, or until onion is translucent. Return lamb to the pan, and add stock, ginger, cinnamon, prunes, and apricots. Bring to a boil, cover the pan, and bake for 1 hour.
4. Remove the pan from the oven, and add carrots and sweet potato. Bake for an additional 45 minutes. Add squash, and bake for an additional 30–40 minutes, or until lamb and vegetables are tender. Season to taste with salt and pepper, and serve immediately, sprinkling each serving with cilantro, if using.

Note: The dish can be prepared up to 2 days in advance and refrigerated, tightly covered. Reheat it, covered, in a 350°F oven for 20–25 minutes, or until hot.

Variation:

- Substitute beef for the lamb; the cooking time will remain the same.

You might think that sautéing onion and garlic at the onset of cooking a dish is an unnecessary step, but it's really important. This initial cooking removes the bitterness from these assertive vegetables so it won't be transferred to the finished dish.

Basque Lamb Meatballs

The Basque region of the Pyrenees between France and Spain is known for its rustic, hearty fare, and its use of lamb. The robust seasoning gives the dish incredible flavor; serve the meatballs over pasta or a cooked grain.

Yield: 4–6 servings | **Active time:** 20 minutes | **Start to finish:** 1 hour

¼ cup olive oil
2 large onions, peeled and chopped
6 garlic cloves, peeled and minced
¼ pound baked ham, finely chopped
1 green bell pepper, seeds and ribs removed, chopped
2 tablespoons smoked Spanish paprika
½ teaspoon dried thyme
1½ cups Beef Stock (recipe on page 24) or purchased stock, divided
½ cup dry sherry
1 (14.5-ounce) can diced tomatoes, undrained
Crushed red pepper flakes to taste
Vegetable oil spray
1 large egg
⅔ cup plain bread crumbs
1 pound ground lamb
Salt and freshly ground black pepper to taste

1. Heat olive oil in a large skillet over medium-high heat. Add onions and garlic, and cook, stirring frequently, for 3 minutes, or until onions are translucent. Remove ⅓ of mixture, and set aside. Add ham and bell pepper, and cook for 3 minutes, stirring frequently. Stir in paprika and thyme and cook for 1 minute, stirring constantly.
2. Add 1¼ cups stock, sherry, tomatoes, and red pepper flakes. Bring to a boil and simmer sauce, uncovered, for 15 minutes, stirring occasionally.
3. Preheat the oven broiler, line a rimmed baking sheet with heavy-duty aluminum foil, and spray the foil with vegetable oil spray.

4. While sauce simmers, whisk egg and remaining ¼ cup stock in a mixing bowl, add bread crumbs, and mix well. Add reserved onion mixture and lamb to the mixing bowl, season to taste with salt and pepper, and mix well again. Make mixture into 1½-inch meatballs, and arrange meatballs on the prepared pan. Spray tops of meatballs with vegetable oil spray.
5. Broil meatballs 6 inches from the broiler element, turning them with tongs to brown all sides. Remove meatballs from the baking pan with a slotted spoon, and add meatballs to sauce. Bring to a boil, and simmer meatballs, covered, over low heat, turning occasionally with a slotted spoon, for 15 minutes or until meatballs are cooked through and no longer pink.

Note: The lamb mixture can be prepared up to 1 day in advance and refrigerated, tightly covered. Also, the dish can be cooked up to 2 days in advance and refrigerated, tightly covered. Reheat it in a 350°F oven, covered, for 15–20 minutes, or until hot.

Variations:

- Change the lamb to ground chuck.
- Substitute uncooked pork sausage for some of the ground lamb.

Chapter 8:

Crusty Creations: Luscious Breads to Serve with Soups and Stews

Freshly baked bread is a treat at any meal, so I've included some of my favorite recipes in this chapter of *$3 Soups and Stews.* I believe that some sort of bread is almost mandatory when you're serving a liquid dish for dinner.

For a soup, the carbohydrate serves as crunchy foil to add textural contrast. For a stew, in addition to adding that contrast, it can be a way to enjoy every drop of the luscious gravy; no one makes a fuss if you dab a corner of bread into a sauce!

The chapter starts out with a selection of traditional yeast breads, but the majority of recipes are for quick breads and muffins that need no kneading, or time to rise, either. These easy recipes can be prepared as you start to simmer a soup, and they'll be ready in less than an hour.

MIXING WITH MASTERY

While cooking is a form of art, when it comes to baking, science class enters the equation as well. These are general pointers on procedures to be used for all genres of baked goods:

- **Measure accurately.** Measure dry ingredients in dry measuring cups, which are plastic or metal and come in sizes of ¼, ⅓, ½, and 1 cup. Spoon dry ingredients from the container or canister into the measuring cup, and then sweep the top with a straight edge, such as the back of a knife or a spatula, to measure it properly. Do not dip the cup into the canister or tap it on the counter to produce a level surface. These methods pack down the dry ingredients and can increase the actual volume by up to 10 percent. Tablespoons and teaspoons should also be leveled; a rounded ½ teaspoon can really measure almost 1 teaspoon. If a box or can does not have a straight edge built in, then level the excess in the spoon back into the container with the back of a knife. Measure liquids in liquid measures, which come in different sizes, but are transparent glass or plastic and have lines on the sides. To accurately measure liquids, place the measuring cup on a flat counter, and bend down to read the marked level.

- **Create consistent temperature.** All ingredients should be at room temperature unless otherwise indicated. Having all ingredients at the same temperature makes it easier to combine them into a smooth, homogeneous mixture. Adding cold liquid to a dough or batter can cause the batter to lose its unified structure by making the fat rigid.

- **Preheat the oven.** Some ovens can take up to 25 minutes to reach a high temperature, such as 450°F. The minimum heating time should be 15 minutes.

- **Plan ahead.** Read the recipe thoroughly, and assemble all your ingredients. This means that you have accounted for all ingredients required for a recipe in advance, so you don't get to a step and realize you must improvise. Assembling in advance also lessens the risk of over-mixing dough or batters, as the mixer drones on while you search for a spice or a bag of chips.

If you're in a hurry to begin a batter, you can grate the butter through the large holes of a box grater. But do not soften butter in a microwave oven. It will become too soft.

MARVELOUS MUFFINS AND EASY QUICK BREADS

Muffins and quick breads are being discussed together because the batters are identical in preparation and they're interchangeable; the only difference is the amount of time and at what temperature they are baked.

Quick breads are so named since they are made with a chemical leavening agent, thus eliminating the time spent waiting for yeast bread doughs to rise. Quick breads can be served as an alternative not only to yeast-raised breads, but also in place of potatoes or rice as a base for stews or other braised dishes. Leftover muffins can be used to create a bread pudding, and leftover quick bread can be turned into a wonderful French toast or stuffing (by first toasting the cubes).

Baked Good	Time	Temperature
Standard muffins	18–22 minutes	400°F
Oversized muffins	20–25 minutes	375°F
Quick breads	45 minutes–1 hour	355°F

YEASTY MATTERS

Many cooks are afraid of working with yeast, so they do not consider making yeast-risen breads. But the whole process could not be easier, and this section provides a primer on how to work with this live leavening agent.

All bread depends on the interaction of some sort of flour, liquid, and leavening agent. Wheat flour contains many substances, including protein, starch, lipids, sugars, and enzymes. When the proteins combine with water, they form gluten. Gluten is both plastic and elastic. These qualities mean that it will hold the carbon dioxide produced by the yeast but will not allow it to escape or break. It is this plasticity that allows bread to rise before it is baked, at which time the structure of the dough solidifies from the heat.

There are two types of yeast—dry (or granulated) yeast and fresh (or compressed) yeast. Yeast is an organic leavening agent, which means that it must be "alive" in order to be effective. The yeast can be killed by overly high temperatures and, conversely, cold temperatures can inhibit the yeast's action. That is why dry yeast should be refrigerated. It will keep for several months, while fresh yeast is quite perishable and can be held under refrigeration for only 7 to 10 days. The fast-rising yeasts are all dry, and they do cut back on the time needed for rising.

To make sure your yeast is alive, you should start with a step called "proofing." Combine the yeast with warm liquid (100–110°F) and a small amount of flour or sugar. If the liquid is any hotter, it might kill the yeast. Either use a meat thermometer to take the temperature, or make sure the liquid feels warm but not hot on the underside of your wrist.

Let the mixture rest at room temperature until a thick surface foam forms, which indicates that the yeast is alive and can be used. If there is no foam, the yeast is dead and should be discarded. After your proofing is successful, you are ready to make the dough.

Kneading is the process of working dough to make it pliable, so it will hold the gas bubbles from the leavening agent and expand when heated. Kneading is done with a pressing-folding-turning action. Press down into the dough with the heels of both hands, then push your hands away from your body. Fold the dough in half, and give it a quarter turn; then repeat the process.

Basic French Bread

This easy recipe is foolproof; I've been making it for years. For a yeast bread, it's also relatively quick to make.

Yield: 1 loaf | **Active time:** 20 minutes | **Start to finish:** 3 hours

1 (1/4-ounce) package active dry yeast
1 1/4 cups warm water (110–115°F)
1 teaspoon granulated sugar
3 cups bread flour, divided
3/4 teaspoon salt
3 tablespoons cornmeal

1. Combine yeast, water, sugar, and 1/4 cup flour in the bowl of a standard electric mixer, and whisk well to dissolve yeast. Set aside for 5 minutes, or until mixture begins to become foamy.
2. Fit the mixer with the paddle attachment. Add remaining flour and salt, and beat at low speed until flour is incorporated to form a soft dough.
3. Place the dough hook on the mixer, and knead dough at medium speed for 2 minutes. Raise the speed to high, and knead for an additional 3–4 minutes, or until dough is springy and elastic. If kneading by hand, it will take about 10–12 minutes. Oil a mixing bowl, and add dough, turning it to make sure top is oiled. Cover bowl with a sheet of plastic wrap, and place it in a warm spot for 1–2 hours, or until dough is doubled in bulk.
4. Lightly oil a baking sheet and sprinkle the center with cornmeal. Punch down dough, and transfer it to a floured surface. Roll or pat dough into a 12 x 6-inch rectangle. Roll dough up tightly from the 12-inch side; shape dough so that ends come to a point. Transfer dough to prepared baking sheet, placing seam down. Cover dough with plastic wrap, and let rise until doubled in bulk, about 45 minutes –1 hour.
5. Preheat the oven to 425°F, and place a low metal pan on the bottom of the oven as it preheats.
6. Slash top of bread in 3 places with a sharp knife. Add 3/4 cup water to the hot pan in the oven. Bake bread for 20–30 minutes, or until it's golden brown and sounds hollow when tapped.

7. Remove the pan from the oven, and cool bread on a rack.

Note: The recipe can be doubled.

The right temperature is necessary for dough to rise. There are some tricks to creating a warm enough temperature in a cold kitchen. Set a foil-covered electric heating pad on low, and put the bowl of dough on the foil; put the bowl in the dishwasher and set it for just the drying cycle; put the bowl in your gas oven to benefit from the warmth from the pilot light; put the bowl in a cold oven over a large pan of boiling-hot water.

Basic Focaccia

Italian focaccia, pronounced *foe-KAH-cha,* is one of the world's great nibble foods, as well as being flat so it's perfect for splitting into a sandwich. This recipe makes a large pan, and for far less money than boutique bakeries charge for a small section.

Yield: 1 loaf (11 x 17 inches) | **Active time:** 20 minutes | **Start to finish:** 3½ hours

3 (¼-ounce) packages active dry yeast
2¼ cups warm water (110–115°F)
1 tablespoon granulated sugar
7 cups all-purpose flour, plus additional if necessary, divided
½ cup extra-virgin olive oil, divided
1½ teaspoons salt
Coarse salt and freshly ground black pepper for sprinkling

1. Combine yeast, water, sugar, and ¼ cup flour in the bowl of a standard electric mixer, and whisk well to dissolve yeast. Set aside for 5 minutes, or until mixture begins to become foamy.
2. Fit the mixer with the paddle attachment. Add ⅓ cup oil, remaining flour, and salt, and beat at low speed until flour is incorporated to form a soft dough.
3. Place the dough hook on the mixer, and knead dough at medium speed for 2 minutes. Raise the speed to high, and knead for an additional 3–4 minutes, or until dough forms a soft ball and is springy. If kneading by hand, it will take about 10–12 minutes. Oil a mixing bowl, and add dough, turning it to make sure top is oiled. Cover bowl with a sheet of plastic wrap, and place it in a warm spot for 1–2 hours, or until dough is doubled in bulk.
4. Preheat the oven to 450°F, and oil an 11 x 17-inch baking sheet. Gently press dough into the prepared pan; allow dough to rest 5 minutes if difficult to work with. Cover the pan with a sheet of oiled plastic wrap, and let rise in a warm place until doubled in bulk, about 30 minutes.
5. Make indentations in dough at 1-inch intervals with oiled fingertips. Drizzle with remaining oil, and sprinkle with coarse salt and pepper. Bake in lower third of oven until deep golden on top and pale golden on bottom, 25–30 minutes. Transfer bread to a rack and serve warm or at room temperature.

Note: This amount of dough is about the maximum that a home standard mixer can make, so the recipe cannot be increased. However, it can be made smaller proportionally.

Variations:

- Sprinkle the top with ¼ cup of a chopped fresh herb, such as rosemary, basil, oregano, or some combination.
- Spread sautéed onions or fennel across the top of the dough before baking.
- Sprinkle the top with ¾ cup freshly grated Parmesan cheese.
- Sprinkle the top with ¾ cup chopped black oil-cured olives.
- Soak 4 garlic cloves, peeled and minced, in the olive oil for 2 hours before making the dough. Either strain and discard garlic, or leave it in if you really like things garlicky.

> Kosher salt is a variation on sea salt. It has a coarse texture, but is much less expensive than sea salt.

No-Knead White Bread

Starting in about 2007, many cookbook authors and food writers began breaking through the hesitancy of making yeast bread by formulating recipes that would succeed *without* the elbow grease necessary for proper kneading. I played around with a number of these; some were much more successful than others. Here's one, based on a recipe by Mark Bittman from the *New York Times,* that I like a lot.

Yield: 1 loaf | **Active time:** 10 minutes | **Start to finish:** 5½ hours

1 (¼ ounce) package active dry yeast
1½ cups warm water (110–115°F)
2 teaspoons granulated sugar
3 cups bread flour, divided
1 teaspoon salt

1. Combine yeast, water, sugar, and ¼ cup flour in a mixing bowl, and whisk well to dissolve yeast. Set aside for 5 minutes, or until mixture begins to become foamy.
2. Add remaining flour and salt, and stir well; the dough will be loose and shaggy. Cover the bowl loosely with plastic wrap. Set bowl in a warm location, and allow dough to rise for 4 hours.
3. Scrape dough out of the mixing bowl, and place it on a well-oiled surface. Using oiled hands, form the dough into a ball, and cover it loosely with plastic wrap. Allow dough to rest for 30 minutes.
4. Preheat the oven to 450°F, and place a 4–6-quart roasting pan in the oven as it preheats. Carefully place dough ball into the hot pan, cover the pan with its lid or a sheet of aluminum foil, and bake bread for 30 minutes. Uncover the pan, and bake for an additional 20–30 minutes, or until bread is brown and sounds hollow when tapped.
5. Remove the pan from the oven, and cool bread on a rack.

Note: This recipe can be doubled successfully.

Variations:

- Add 2 tablespoons of a chopped herb, such as rosemary, oregano, or dill.
- Add ½ cup chopped oil-cured black olives.
- Add ¼ cup freshly grated Parmesan cheese or grated cheddar cheese.

Cornmeal Cheese Muffins

Savory muffins are wonderful both at breakfast and as a dinner bread, and I like the combination of corn with the flavorful cheese.

Yield: 12 muffins | **Active time:** 10 minutes | **Start to finish:** 30 minutes

1 cup all-purpose flour
1 cup yellow cornmeal
1 tablespoon baking powder
1 tablespoon granulated sugar
½ teaspoon salt
½ teaspoon baking soda
1 cup buttermilk, shaken well
1 large egg
5 tablespoons unsalted butter, melted
1 cup grated cheddar cheese, divided

1. Preheat the oven to 400°F, and grease a 12-cup muffin pan; you can also use paper liners.
2. Combine flour, cornmeal, baking powder, sugar, salt, and baking soda in a large mixing bowl, and whisk well. Add buttermilk, egg, butter, and ⅔ cup cheese. Stir gently to wet flour, but do not whisk until smooth; batter should be lumpy. Fill each prepared cup ⅔ full, and sprinkle with remaining cheese.
3. Bake muffins for 18–20 minutes, or until a toothpick inserted in the center comes out clean. Place muffin pan on a cooling rack for 10 minutes, then serve.

Note: Muffins can be served hot or at room temperature.

Variations:

- Substitute jalapeño Jack for the cheddar cheese for a spicy, Southwestern muffin, and add ¼ teaspoon cayenne pepper to batter.
- Add 1 tablespoon Italian seasoning and 1 garlic clove, peeled and pushed through a garlic press, to batter.

Parmesan Herb Muffins

Savory muffins can replace expensive breads on your dinner table, and because no yeast is used, they can be on the table quickly.

Yield: 12 muffins | **Active time:** 10 minutes | **Start to finish:** 30 minutes

1½ cups all-purpose flour
2 teaspoons baking powder
2 teaspoons Italian seasoning
½ teaspoon baking soda
½ teaspoon salt
Freshly ground black pepper to taste
¾ cup whole milk
2 large eggs, beaten
½ cup olive oil
3 tablespoons chopped fresh parsley
1 cup freshly grated Parmesan cheese, divided
2 garlic cloves, peeled and minced

1. Preheat the oven to 400°F, and grease a 12-cup muffin pan; you can also use paper liners.
2. Combine flour, baking powder, Italian seasoning, baking soda, salt, and pepper in a large mixing bowl, and whisk well. Add milk, eggs, oil, parsley, ⅔ cup cheese, and garlic. Stir gently to wet flour, but do not whisk until smooth; batter should be lumpy. Fill each prepared cup ⅔ full, and sprinkle with remaining cheese.
3. Bake muffins for 18–20 minutes, or until a toothpick inserted in the center comes out clean. Place muffin pan on a cooling rack for 10 minutes, then serve.

Note: Muffins can be served hot or at room temperature.

Variations:

- Add ½ cup sun-dried tomatoes packed in olive oil, drained and chopped. Use the olive oil from the tomatoes as part of the oil for the recipe.
- Substitute dried oregano for the Italian seasoning, and add 1 tablespoon grated lemon zest.

Basic Beer Bread

I love beer bread because it has the same yeasty aroma and flavor as a rustic yeast bread, but it's so easy to make. In addition to serving it at dinner, I use it in place of sandwich bread.

Yield: 1 loaf | **Active time:** 10 minutes | **Start to finish:** 50 minutes

3½ cups all-purpose flour
1 teaspoon baking powder
½ teaspoon salt
½ teaspoon baking soda
1 large egg, beaten lightly
1 (12-ounce) can lager beer

1. Preheat the oven to 350°F, and grease a 9 x 5 x 3-inch loaf pan.
2. Combine flour, baking powder, salt, and baking soda in a large mixing bowl, and whisk well. Add egg and beer, and stir until batter is just combined; batter should be lumpy. Scrape batter into the prepared pan.
3. Bake bread for 40–45 minutes, or until a toothpick inserted in the center comes out clean. Place pan on a cooling rack for 5 minutes, then turn bread out of the pan and serve.

Note: Bread can be served hot or at room temperature.

Variations:

- For a sweeter bread, add ½ cup granulated sugar.
- Add ½ cup chopped sun-dried tomatoes or ½ cup chopped oil-cured black olives, or ¼ cup of each.
- Add ½ cup chopped scallions, white parts and 3 inches of green tops.
- Add ¼ cup chopped fresh dill.

Irish Soda Bread

This hearty and rustic bread is one of the easiest to make, and it comes to the table looking pretty with a bright, shiny crust.

Yield: 2 (6-inch) loaves | **Active time:** 10 minutes | **Start to finish:** 50 minutes

4 cups all-purpose flour
2 tablespoons granulated sugar
1½ teaspoons baking soda
1 teaspoon salt
1¾ cups buttermilk, shaken well
2 tablespoons unsalted butter, melted

1. Preheat the oven to 375°F, and grease and flour a baking sheet.
2. Combine flour, sugar, baking soda, and salt in a large mixing bowl, and whisk well. Add buttermilk, and stir until batter is just combined; batter should be lumpy. Transfer dough to a well-floured surface, and knead with floured hands for 1 minute, or until dough is less sticky.
3. Divide dough in half, and pat each half into a 6-inch round on the prepared baking sheet. Cut an X ½ inch deep on top of each round, and brush tops with butter.
4. Bake bread for 35–40 minutes, or until tops are golden. Transfer loaves to a cooling rack with a wide spatula, and cool for at least 15 minutes.

Note: The bread can be served the day it is made, but it slices more easily if kept, wrapped in plastic wrap, at room temperature for 1 day, and up to 4 days.

Variations:

- Add 1 cup raisins to dough, or 1 cup any chopped dried fruit, like dried apples or pitted dates.
- Add ½ cup chopped scallions, white parts and 3 inches of green tops.
- Add 2 tablespoons crushed caraway seeds or fennel seeds.

Whole Wheat Oatmeal Soda Bread

Here's a variation on soda bread that adds heart-healthy grains to your diet as well as their innate flavors and aromas to the bread.

Yield: 2 (7-inch) loaves | **Active time:** 10 minutes | **Start to finish:** 50 minutes

2¼ cups all-purpose flour
2 cups whole wheat flour
1¼ cups old-fashioned rolled oats, divided
2 teaspoons baking soda
1 teaspoon baking powder
½ teaspoon salt
2 cups buttermilk
1 large egg, beaten
2 tablespoons unsalted butter, melted

1. Preheat the oven to 375°F, and grease and flour a baking sheet.
2. Combine all-purpose flour, whole wheat flour, 1 cup oats, baking soda, baking powder, and salt in a large mixing bowl, and whisk well. Add buttermilk and egg, and stir until batter is just combined; batter should be lumpy. Transfer dough to a well-floured surface, and knead with floured hands for 1 minute, or until dough is less sticky.
3. Divide dough in half, and pat each half into a 7-inch round on the prepared baking sheet. Cut an X ½ inch deep on top of each round, and brush tops with butter. Sprinkle loaves with remaining ¼ cup oats.
4. Bake bread for 35–40 minutes, or until tops are golden. Transfer loaves to a cooling rack with a wide spatula, and cool for at least 15 minutes.

Note: The bread can be served the day it is made, but it slices more easily if kept, wrapped in plastic wrap, at room temperature for 1 day, and up to 4 days.

Basic Herb Quick Bread

In addition to being a delicious accompaniment to any meal, this loaf also can be transformed into savory French toast for a brunch; top it with a marinara sauce.

Yield: 1 loaf | **Active time:** 10 minutes | **Start to finish:** 1 hour

3 cups all-purpose flour
2 tablespoons granulated sugar
2 tablespoons baking powder
2 tablespoons herbes de Provence
1 teaspoon salt
Freshly ground black pepper to taste
2 large eggs, beaten
1¼ cups whole milk
⅓ cup olive oil

1. Preheat the oven to 350°F, and grease a 9 x 5 x 3-inch loaf pan.
2. Combine flour, sugar, baking powder, herbes de Provence, salt, and pepper in a large mixing bowl, and whisk well. Add eggs, milk, and oil, and stir until batter is just combined; batter should be lumpy. Scrape batter into the prepared pan.
3. Bake bread for 50–55 minutes, or until a toothpick inserted in the center comes out clean. Place pan on a cooling rack for 10 minutes, then turn bread out of the pan and serve.

Note: Bread can be served hot or at room temperature.

Variations:

- Substitute Italian seasoning for the herbes de Provence for an equally complex but more assertive flavor.
- Add 3 tablespoons chopped fresh parsley.
- Omit the herbs and add ¼ cup chopped oil-cured black olives.

Sun-Dried Tomato Herb Quick Bread

This aromatic, flavorful quick bread makes a wonderful grilled cheese sandwich if sliced thin and toasted with some fontina or mozzarella cheese in the center.

Yield: 1 loaf | **Active time:** 10 minutes | **Start to finish:** 1 hour

- 2 cups all-purpose flour
- 1 tablespoon baking powder
- 1 tablespoon herbes de Provence
- ½ teaspoon salt
- ¼ teaspoon freshly ground pepper
- 1 cup whole milk
- ⅓ cup olive oil
- 1 large egg, beaten
- ½ cup freshly grated Parmesan cheese
- ¼ cup finely chopped sun-dried tomatoes packed in oil
- 2 tablespoons chopped fresh parsley
- 1 tablespoon chopped fresh herbs (oregano, basil, marjoram, or some combination)

1. Preheat the oven to 350°F, and grease a 9 x 5 x 3-inch loaf pan.
2. Combine flour, baking powder, herbes de Provence, salt, and pepper in a large mixing bowl, and whisk well. Add milk, oil, egg, cheese, sun-dried tomatoes, parsley, and herbs. Stir until batter is just combined; batter should be lumpy. Scrape batter into the prepared pan.
3. Bake bread for 50–55 minutes, or until a toothpick inserted in the center comes out clean. Place pan on a cooling rack for 10 minutes, then turn bread out of the pan and serve.

Note: Bread can be served hot or at room temperature.

Buttermilk Biscuits

A true Southern biscuit is a tender, flaky work of art that is incredibly easy to make, and once you have made a batch you will become addicted!

Yield: 20 (2-inch) biscuits | **Active time:** 10 minutes | **Start to finish:** 30 minutes

- 1½ cups cake flour (not self-rising)
- ½ cup all-purpose flour
- 1 tablespoon baking powder
- ½ teaspoon salt
- ½ teaspoon baking soda
- 6 tablespoons vegetable shortening
- ⅔ cup buttermilk
- 3 tablespoons unsalted butter, melted

1. Preheat oven to 425°F, and lightly grease a baking sheet.
2. Sift cake flour, all-purpose flour, baking powder, salt, and baking soda into a large mixing bowl. Cut in the vegetable shortening using a pastry blender, two knives, or your fingertips until mixture resembles coarse meal. Add buttermilk, and stir with a fork until just combined.
3. Transfer mixture to a lightly floured surface, and knead 10 times with the heel of your hand to bring the dough together. Pat dough into a round that is ½ inch thick.
4. Cut dough into 2-inch circles and place them 1 inch apart on the prepared baking sheet. Brush tops with melted butter. Gather scraps and pat into a circle again to cut out more biscuits. Repeat until all dough is used.
5. Bake for 18–20 minutes, or until cooked through and golden brown. Serve immediately.

Note: The biscuits can be cut out up to 1 hour in advance. Do not bake them until just prior to serving.

Variations:

- For cheese biscuits, add ½ cup grated cheddar, Swiss, or Gruyère cheese to the dough.
- For breakfast biscuits, combine ⅓ cup firmly packed dark brown sugar, ½ cup toasted chopped nuts, and ½ teaspoon ground cinnamon in a small bowl, and pat the mixture onto the top of biscuits before baking.

Flour is usually classified by the species of wheat from which it's ground, and Southern species produce what is called "soft flour" because it has a low protein count. In the South biscuits are made with the local all-purpose flour, but I specify cake flour to ensure that the protein count is low.

Cornbread

If you have a well-seasoned cast-iron skillet around, you can bake the cornbread right in it, and then bring it to the table. This is an all-purpose recipe that really goes with any entree and is as at home on the breakfast table as on the dinner table.

Yield: 6–8 servings | **Active time:** 10 minutes | **Start to finish:** 30 minutes

- 1 cup yellow cornmeal
- 1 cup all-purpose flour
- 2 tablespoons granulated sugar
- 1½ teaspoons baking powder
- ½ teaspoon baking soda
- ¼ teaspoon salt
- 2 large eggs
- ¾ cup buttermilk
- ½ cup creamed corn
- 5 tablespoons unsalted butter, melted

1. Preheat the oven to 425°F. Generously grease a 9-inch-square pan.
2. Whisk together cornmeal, flour, sugar, baking powder, baking soda, and salt in a large mixing bowl. Whisk together eggs, buttermilk, creamed corn, and butter in a small bowl. Add buttermilk mixture to cornmeal mixture, and stir batter until just blended.
3. Heat the greased pan in the oven for 3 minutes, or until it is very hot. Remove the pan from the oven, and spread batter in it evenly. Bake cornbread in the middle of the oven for 15 minutes, or until top is pale golden and the sides begin to pull away from the edges of the pan.
4. Allow cornbread to cool for 5 minutes, then turn it out onto a rack. Cut into pieces, and serve hot or at room temperature.

Note: The cornbread is best eaten within a few hours of baking.

Appendix A:

Metric Conversion Tables

The scientifically precise calculations needed for baking are not necessary when cooking conventionally. The tables in this appendix are designed for general cooking. If making conversions for baking, grab your calculator and compute the exact figure.

CONVERTING OUNCES TO GRAMS

The numbers in the following table are approximate. To reach the exact quantity of grams, multiply the number of ounces by 28.35.

Ounces	Grams
1 ounce	30 grams
2 ounces	60 grams
3 ounces	85 grams
4 ounces	115 grams
5 ounces	140 grams
6 ounces	180 grams
7 ounces	200 grams
8 ounces	225 grams
9 ounces	250 grams
10 ounces	285 grams
11 ounces	300 grams
12 ounces	340 grams
13 ounces	370 grams
14 ounces	400 grams
15 ounces	425 grams
16 ounces	450 grams

CONVERTING QUARTS TO LITERS

The numbers in the following table are approximate. To reach the exact amount of liters, multiply the number of quarts by 0.95.

Quarts	Liter
1 cup (1/4 quart)	1/4 liter
1 pint (1/2 quart)	1/2 liter
1 quart	1 liter
2 quarts	2 liters
2 1/2 quarts	2 1/2 liters
3 quarts	2 3/4 liters
4 quarts	3 3/4 liters
5 quarts	4 3/4 liters
6 quarts	5 1/2 liters
7 quarts	6 1/2 liters
8 quarts	7 1/2 liters

CONVERTING POUNDS TO GRAMS AND KILOGRAMS

The numbers in the following table are approximate. To reach the exact quantity of grams, multiply the number of pounds by 453.6.

Pounds	Grams; Kilograms
1 pound	450 grams
1 1/2 pounds	675 grams
2 pounds	900 grams
2 1/2 pounds	1,125 grams; 1 1/4 kilograms
3 pounds	1,350 grams
3 1/2 pounds	1,500 grams; 1 1/2 kilograms
4 pounds	1,800 grams
4 1/2 pounds	2 kilograms
5 pounds	2 1/4 kilograms
5 1/2 pounds	2 1/2 kilograms
6 pounds	2 3/4 kilograms
6 1/2 pounds	3 kilograms
7 pounds	3 1/4 kilograms
7 1/2 pounds	3 1/2 kilograms
8 pounds	3 3/4 kilograms

CONVERTING FAHRENHEIT TO CELSIUS

The numbers in the following table are approximate. To reach the exact temperature, subtract 32 from the Fahrenheit reading, multiply the number by 5, and then divide by 9.

Degrees Fahrenheit	Degrees Celsius
170°F	77°C
180°F	82°C
190°F	88°C
200°F	95°C
225°F	110°C
250°F	120°C
300°F	150°C
325°F	165°C
350°F	180°C
375°F	190°C
400°F	205°C
425°F	220°C
450°F	230°C
475°F	245°C
500°F	260°C

CONVERTING INCHES TO CENTIMETERS

The numbers in the following table are approximate. To reach the exact number of centimeters, multiply the number of inches by 2.54.

Inches	Centimeters
½ inch	1.5 centimeters
1 inch	2.5 centimeters
2 inches	5 centimeters
3 inches	8 centimeters
4 inches	10 centimeters
5 inches	13 centimeters
6 inches	15 centimeters
7 inches	18 centimeters
8 inches	20 centimeters
9 inches	23 centimeters
10 inches	25 centimeters
11 inches	28 centimeters
12 inches	30 centimeters

Appendix B:

Table of Weights and Measures of Common Ingredients

Food	Quantity	Yield
Apples	1 pound	2½–3 cups sliced
Avocado	1 pound	1 cup mashed
Bananas	1 medium	1 cup sliced
Bell peppers	1 pound	3–4 cups sliced
Blueberries	1 pound	3⅓ cups
Butter	¼ pound (1 stick)	8 tablespoons
Cabbage	1 pound	4 cups packed shredded
Carrots	1 pound	3 cups diced or sliced
Chocolate, morsels	12 ounces	2 cups
Chocolate, bulk	1 ounce	3 tablespoons grated
Cocoa powder	1 ounce	¼ cup
Coconut, flaked	7 ounces	2½ cups
Cream	½ pint (1 cup)	2 cups whipped
Cream cheese	8 ounces	1 cup
Flour	1 pound	4 cups
Lemons	1 medium	3 tablespoons juice
Lemons	1 medium	2 teaspoons zest
Milk	1 quart	4 cups
Molasses	12 ounces	1½ cups
Mushrooms	1 pound	5 cups sliced
Onions	1 medium	½ cup chopped
Peaches	1 pound	2 cups sliced
Peanuts	5 ounces	1 cup
Pecans	6 ounces	1½ cups
Pineapple	1 medium	3 cups diced
Potatoes	1 pound	3 cups sliced
Raisins	1 pound	3 cups
Rice	1 pound	2 to 2½ cups raw
Spinach	1 pound	¾ cup cooked
Squash, summer	1 pound	3½ cups sliced
Strawberries	1 pint	1½ cups sliced

Food	Quantity	Yield
Sugar, brown	1 pound	2¼ cups, packed
Sugar, confectioners'	1 pound	4 cups
Sugar, granulated	1 pound	2¼ cups
Tomatoes	1 pound	1½ cups pulp
Walnuts	4 ounces	1 cup

TABLE OF LIQUID MEASUREMENTS

Dash	=	less than ⅛ teaspoon
3 teaspoons	=	1 tablespoon
2 tablespoons	=	1 ounce
8 tablespoons	=	½ cup
2 cups	=	1 pint
1 quart	=	2 pints
1 gallon	=	4 quarts

Index

Page references at main subject refer to general discussions on topic.